LITERARY S

Reviews

"excellent … full of interesting facts which will encourage an exploration of Surrey very shortly!" (Rosemary Culley, Alliance of Literary Societies)

"will appeal to anyone interested in how the countryside and history of the county have influenced some of Britain's most respected writers" (*Woking News & Mail*)

"so pleasant to read and I loved all the anecdotes" (Susannah Fullerton, President, Jane Austen Society of Australia)

"Jane Austen is only one of many writers whose connections with Surrey are dealt with…. [Jacqueline's] riposte to Charlotte Brontë's naive accusation that there is 'no open country–no fresh air–no blue hill–no bonny beck!' in *Pride and Prejudice* would lift the heart of any Janeite" (David Selwyn, News Letter of the Jane Austen Society)

"chronicles a whole host of writers who held the county close to their hearts. Focusing on the powerful effect of Surrey on their life and work, the volume covers luminaries from Matthew Arnold and Lewis Carroll to EM Forster and HG Wells" (*Elmbridge Lifestyle*)

"The Places to Visit sections at the end of every chapter tantalise with suggestive layers of significance; they also contain useful information (directions, phone numbers and opening hours) that allows the reader to use this book as a guide on a tour around the county to places of literary significance. *Literary Surrey* is an interesting book, attractively produced, and entertainingly written… well worth the read" (Lorna Clark, *The Burney Letter*)

"It may not be as hallowed as Shakespeare Country or Austen Country but Jacqueline has proved Surrey has an authorial history to be proud of" (Paul Fleckney, *Walton and Weybridge Guardian*)

"explores the rich literary heritage of the county, including Surbiton and Kingston" (Sarah Loveridge, *The Kingston Informer*)

"a surprisingly detailed overview for those interested in the history of the area and its relation to Wells' masterwork…. Each chapter includes excellent notations (including online references)…." (Charles Keller, The HG Wells Society Newsletter)

"a lively exploration of the time spent and the work written in Surrey by authors from John Evelyn and Fanny Burney to HG Wells and EM Forster" (*Farnham Herald*)

Excerpts from *Literary Surrey* (entitled 'Riding Out with William Cobbett' and 'The Surrey Years of EM Forster') have appeared in *This England*.

LITERARY SURREY

Jacqueline Banerjee

Literary Surrey

First published 2005

This edition includes all corrections up to November 2007

Typeset and published by John Owen Smith
19 Kay Crescent, Headley Down, Hampshire GU35 8AH

Tel: 01428 712892 – Fax: 08700 516554
wordsmith@johnowensmith.co.uk
www.johnowensmith.co.uk

ISBN 978-1873855-50-8 (1-873855-50-8)

Printed and bound by CPI Antony Rowe, Eastbourne

For Caroline, Sarah and Alexander

Sheridan's Walk at Polesden Lacey.
The plinth is inscribed with a passage from Alexander Pope's Essay on Man.

Contents

Illustrations

Every effort has been made to contact the original copyright holders. Please let me know if I have missed anyone. Illustrations not otherwise attributed are from my own photographs.

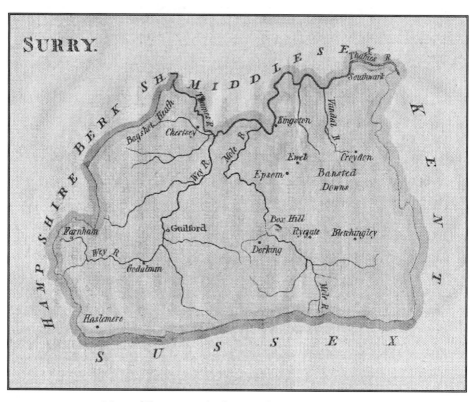

Map of Surrey in the late eighteenth century,
showing the principal rivers and towns, and bordering counties.
Box Hill is also shown.

Preface

Oddly enough, this book started with a plumbing problem. Busy with the caulking tape under the cistern, the plumber suddenly mentioned the name Forster. I pricked up my ears. Apparently, the running battle he'd been talking about, the one with his neighbour over some plaque or other, had nothing to do with his pipe-work at all. It was over which of their houses E.M. Forster had been living in when he wrote *A Passage to India*. And this was just down the road to us! It was a revelation to me.

Of course, I knew Surrey was steeped in history. All the home counties are, I suppose, thanks to being on London's doorstep. But Surrey does seem rather special. Even after the last shake-up of county boundaries,[1] it still has within its postal district the coronation stone of the first Saxon kings at Kingston-on-Thames, and the birthplace of democracy at Runnymede where King John was forced into a corner by his angry barons and affixed his royal seal to the Magna Carta. Other old Surrey towns like Kew and Epsom are also known to people all over the world, for entirely different reasons. And almost anywhere in Surrey, a stretch of crumbling wall or a curious street name will suddenly evoke a wonderfully rich historical past.

But I'd never thought about this county's literary past. After all, it has no Stratford, no "Brontë country" or "Hardy country," no Lake District. Perhaps it lies too close to the capital, where writers and literary pilgrims alike have always been drawn to certain well-defined areas like Fleet Street, Southwark and Bloomsbury. Besides, isn't there something prosaic, not to mention materialistic, about its comfortable, stockbroker-belt image?

Nevertheless, as I began to discover, Surrey has been host to some of our best-loved literary figures, and some of the great masterpieces of our literature have been produced here.

For, after all, it has plenty to offer the creative mind. "Leafy Surrey" is still not a myth or a misnomer. This is the most thickly wooded county in England,[2] and writers as different and far apart in time as the diarist John Evelyn and Forster himself have shared a delight in its ancient woodland. Then there are Surrey's rivers, from the busy Thames itself to the Wey, the aptly-named burrowing Mole, the beautiful Tillingbourne, and the Hogsmill, beloved of the Pre-Raphaelites John Millais and William Holman Hunt. The great liberal humanist Matthew Arnold was not alone in revelling in these rivers, whether by bathing in them, rowing on them or fishing along them. Best of all, there are Surrey's views and vistas. As well as the vantage point of Box Hill, scene of the famously fraught expedition in Jane Austen's

Emma, Surrey has Leith Hill and Hindhead, with the North Downs and the Weald at their feet. Little wonder, then, that over the years many writers have been drawn here.

What they wrote in this lovely landscape depended partly on the stage of their careers when they were here. H.G. Wells, for instance, came to stay in Surrey as a young man on the brink of success, not very fit but still fizzing with energy. Eager to build up his health, he threw himself into boating, cycling, even the losing battle with slugs in the garden—and into writing his extraordinarily inventive "scientific romances." Others, including William Cobbett who was born and raised here, found more of their material in the natural world, and never lost their passion for it. Then there were those, like George Meredith, who lived through the years of their maturity here, finding the Surrey setting a poignant background for poetry and novels about the struggles of the human heart. As for those who retired here for their more sedate later years, like George Eliot and her partner G.H. Lewes, who took a house in Witley at the end of 1877, the Surrey period was liable to be a time of reflection—of writing essays and letters, perhaps.

Admittedly, there were one or two who wished they were nearer the hum and thrum of the city. The seventeenth-century poet (and later Dean of St Paul's) John Donne, whose secret marriage had cut him off from court life, used his time here for studying the law, but felt increasingly wretched as his exile dragged on. He and his wife moved from her cousin's home at Pyrford Place, Pyrford, to Camberwell and then to Mitcham, at which point, with his growing family dogged by illness and poverty, he more or less gave up on the county. He found himself some lodgings in the Strand to be nearer the centre of power and patronage again. For him, Surrey had become more like a cage or a sickbay than anything else. But then, his circumstances during those years were truly desperate.

Those who found their time in Surrey more congenial are generally remembered with pride by the individual towns and villages whose streets they once walked. Here, the prize must go to Woking, which marked H.G. Wells's fruitful stay in Surrey with a tall, eye-catching steel Martian war-machine in its town centre. Even the bacteria which finally overcome these devastating tripods in *The War of the Worlds* are recalled in a series of mosaics set into the pavement—a unique kind of literary memorial, I should think, and likely to remain so. There are more glimpses of Wells in Woking's new town gate, in murals under a railway bridge and in a pedestrian underpass, and in the local Wetherspoons pub. Shaw's stay in Woking is commemorated in some of those places too. Although Shaw moved around a lot during these years, he completed his "Don Juan" comedy, *Man and Superman,* there in 1903.

Some of Surrey's other literary associations are also celebrated locally, by brass plaques in churches, or blue plaques on houses. The museums of Farnham and Guildford, respectively, do William Cobbett and Lewis Carroll proud, and Haslemere Museum has a whole galaxy of local writers from

Surrey's south-western border to celebrate.[3]   Branch libraries often have interesting collections of material on even the less widely read authors who once lived nearby, and such figures still have a real presence in the neighbourhood. The nineteenth-century satirist Thomas Love Peacock, for instance, needs little introduction in Shepperton, where his old home occupies a prominent place facing Lower Halliford Green, and is graced with a fine peacock weathervane as well as a blue plaque.

In fact, Surrey has such a rich literary heritage that I had to be selective about the authors I covered, mentioning some only in passing, and leaving out a few who perhaps spent less time here, or whose stay here didn't particularly affect their writing or throw light on their writing careers.

For what interests me most is the interaction of mind and place in these authors' works. Knowing the spot in Surrey where, for example, Keats was inspired to complete his first major poem, helps us to appreciate better both the poem and the area—Keat's delight in the River Mole there ("a little river," "a crystal Rill") is particularly infectious.   Similarly, to read of Matthew Arnold's pleasure in walking from Cobham to Weybridge is to warm to the human being behind the humanist, and also to sense the romance of the old Surrey roads. And to imagine Siegfried Sassoon and E.M. Forster standing together at the gates of Ashley Park in Walton-on-Thames, shortly before it was demolished, is to glimpse not only a fruitful literary friendship, but a whole bygone era of great Surrey estates as well.

So, just as we go to Runnymede to feel close to the dawn of civil liberties, we might also go to such places as Box Hill and Cobham, to reflect on the other messages which our culture has sent out into the world—and to enjoy the surroundings with those messages in mind. Of course, it isn't always necessary to set off by road or rail. Although I suggest a few places to visit at the end of each chapter, this isn't really intended as a guidebook. It's for anyone who is interested in the highways and byways of our literature, even if they only wish to travel them in their mind's eye, and from the comfort of their own armchair.[4]

Finally, I'm so grateful to my family and to all the other kind people who have lent their time, advice, information and illustrations to this project, especially to my husband, who has taken me round (and round) Surrey in pursuit of the literary past. Special thanks also to Teruhiko Nagao and Wendy Hughes for their interest and encouragement; to the Rehs Gallery, New York, Devonshire Fine Arts (at antique-maps-online.co.uk) and Ros King at Heaton's of Tisbury; to the artists Tim Frost, Janet Gale and Diane Setek; to the photographers Chris Head and John Powell; to the librarians of King's College, London, for permitting me to copy old frontispieces etc.; to the helpful staff of the Imperial War Museum, London, the Juniper Hall Field Centre, Keats House, Painshill Park, the Surrey History Centre and Wotton House; and above all to John Owen Smith for his patience, kindness and technical expertise and the R.C. Sherriff Rosebriars Trust for their generous publication grant. As I explain at the end of Chapter 10, the Trust was established with the proceeds of the estate of local playwright and screenwriter, R.C. Sherriff. I was thrilled to have the support of one of "my" authors, and I hope I've done him justice here.

Walton-on-Thames, April 2005

Notes to Preface

[1] Surrey's boundaries, like those of other counties, have been redrawn over the years. This study includes some areas which have become a part of Greater London, but still have a Surrey postal address.

[2] Facts and figures are given in "If You Go Down to the Woods Today…," *The Sunday Times*, 25 Nov. 2001, Section I, p.15.

[3] See W.R. Trotter's *The Hilltop Writers: A Victorian Colony among the Surrey Hills*, also published by John Owen Smith (2003). This deals with the many writers, from Tennyson to Sir Arthur Conan Doyle, who spent some time in the south-west corner of Surrey, where the countryside spreads into West Sussex and Hampshire, in the late Victorian period.

[4] With such readers in mind, I haven't completely limited my "Suggested Reading" sections to descriptions of local places. After all, the achievements of those who were born, lived, or wrote here belong to the wider tradition as well. Also, since London is sometimes easier to reach than the other side of the county, I add to the "Places to Visit" sections a few sites there that are of particular interest. Such sites are marked by asterisks. The information in these sections was checked as thoroughly as possible before publication, but situations can change very quickly, and I would be happy to be told of anything that needs correcting.

"There will the river whisp'ring run…" (John Donne, "The Bait")
The Wey at Pyrford, where Donne spent the early years of his marriage

1. John Evelyn, FRS,
A True Surrey Gentleman

John Evelyn in 1689: "I sat for my Picture to Mr Kneller ...
holding my Sylva in my right hand"

What "E" links gunpowder, salad dressing, parks and shampoo? Of course, the chapter heading gives the game away, but it's an intriguing mixture, isn't it?

John Evelyn (1620–1706) is known today almost entirely as a diarist, but that was really just the by-product of an extremely busy and varied life—the life of a man whose motto was "*Omnia explorate; meliora retinete*" (derived from *1 Thessalonians*, 5, 21) or, to put it loosely in more modern terms, "Try out everything, and hang on to the best." Though this wasn't something he publicised himself, Evelyn's family fortunes were founded on gunpowder. As a young man, he travelled widely on the continent, and brought home with him a taste for olive oil based salad-dressings, or, as he called it, an "Oxeloeum of Vinegar, Pepper, and Oyl."[1] Public parks answered two of his requirements: better air quality in urban areas, and refreshment of the soul. As for shampoo, he instituted, for himself at least, a yearly ritual of washing his hair with a warm herbal brew followed by a refreshing rinse with cold spring water.

Evelyn's interests as a writer were no less disparate. Amongst other works on politics, morals, religion, architecture, painting, sculpture, navigation and trade, coins—and salads, of course—he published treatises on the evils of pollution (*Fumifugium*, 1661), the importance of planting trees (*Sylva, or a Discourse of Forest-Trees in His Majestie's Dominions*, 1664), and the delights of gardening (the *Compleat Gard'ner*, a translation from the French, 1693). These three are, as indeed they sound, curiously relevant to modern concerns.

In his public life, Evelyn was equally versatile. His official court appointments involved him in the planning of some of London's landmark buildings, and his connections with the highest in the land meant that he could (for example) not only discover but also bring to the royal attention the famous wood carver Grinling Gibbons, whose work can be seen in St Paul's, Windsor Castle and so on. Although few people realise it, Evelyn's own name is still a household word today. He had a marvellous still room where essences and preserves were prepared, and which so inspired a certain Cyrus Harvey that he honoured Evelyn, along with the slightly later horticulturalist George Crabtree, by using his name for his company: Crabtree and Evelyn.

***

Evelyn was born in 1620 at Wotton (pronounced Wootton) House, just a few miles west of Dorking off the A25 Guildford Road. This was an old moated manor house mentioned in the Domesday Book, which would undergo various alterations over the years, especially at the hands of Evelyn's elder brother George in the mid-seventeenth century, and then again during the period of Gothic Revival in the nineteenth century. This was when a later Evelyn, William John Evelyn, strengthened the lines of the more gently rambling and genuinely old building with an imposing new Tudor/Jacobean façade. Nevertheless, Wotton remains fundamentally the same house and, remarkably, it has stayed in the hands of one family all this time, longer than any other private estate in the whole country—ever since it was first acquired by Evelyn's grandfather in 1579. According to the "Brief History" currently available at the House, the present Lord of the Manor of Wotton, John Patrick Evelyn, inherited Wotton in 1965. Not mentioned there is the fact that this John Evelyn won his own kind of fame by becoming European Junior

Bobsleigh Champion the following year, and twice after that representing Britain at the Olympics. Not something his seventeenth-century ancestor could have foreseen!

Wotton House: "large and antient, suitable to those hospitable times"

Standing in its hollow amid the Surrey hills, the house probably looks more impressive than ever these days. This is because its lease was acquired by the Hayley Group of Conference Centres in 2000. The old building, which had been used for all sorts of purposes since World War II and was really looking quite decrepit, was soon surrounded by scaffolding. It was then thoroughly refurbished inside as well, to produce over a hundred bedrooms, a swimming pool, a spa pool and all the other accoutrements of modern corporate junketing. Inevitably, something of the corporate atmosphere clings to it now, and the brickwork looks a little raw. But out the back is something rare and wonderful, and altogether more like the real thing—for its twenty-acre listed grounds have been at least partially restored too. The ground rises dramatically behind formally patterned flowerbeds with a central fountain (mentioned in the diary), and three flights of steps lead up the slope to a viewpoint at the top. Cut into the space beneath the viewpoint is a striking classical-style grotto. This was all done in consultation with Evelyn, "by digging down the Mountaine" which once came within ten yards of the house, and "flinging it into a rapid streame,"[2] in order to level the flower-bed area and produce a surround for the grotto. So far, the steps up the remaining hill, and the statues at either side of the top two flights, have not been smartened up. This makes for an atmospheric

21

climb, enhanced by the coveys of pheasants, which whirr up from the long grass as visitors approach.

There is no sign, however, of the more exotic species which Evelyn's descendants liked to keep there—including zebras and kangaroos, some of which bounded away to their freedom, startling ramblers who expected to see nothing more bouncy than a bunny!

Not far along the A25, off the Shere Road, is another striking example of Evelyn's ambitious landscaping. Albury Park, which he designed for the Duke of Norfolk, has also been restored, and the Evelyn Terrace with its quarter-of-a-mile yew walk is quite spectacular. The gardens were added to by other hands, but much of Evelyn's original design remains, as do many of the trees planted by his instruction. Little wonder that the major British Library exhibition of 2004–5 on the theme of "The Writer and the Garden" devoted several display cases to Evelyn under the title, "Virtuoso Gardener." Albury House now belongs to the Historic House Retirement Homes Association. The Evelyn Garden itself is only opened twice a year, but the public can walk through part of the grounds to the lovely old Saxon church there, and enjoy the variety of splendid old trees around it, including a Giant Redwood beside the church itself. Evelyn would surely have approved.

The Evelyn Terrace at Albury Park

As a gardening writer, Evelyn is unsurpassed. He saw the garden as a reflection of the Garden of Eden, the nearest man can get to Paradise on earth. Everything in it had meaning for him, particularly its trees aspiring to the heavens, and its evergreens with their suggestion of immortality. And since he conveyed these noble feelings to his readers along with the most helpful and minutely detailed practical advice, even down to which kind of tools to use, he was hugely influential in this sphere.

Nevertheless, many would point to his diary as his greatest gift to posterity. It was discovered by chance over a hundred years after his death by a librarian visiting Wotton House. The story goes that it was found in a laundry basket, but what really happened, it seems, was that the housekeeper simply used such a basket to fetch down some old papers for him. Whatever the exact circumstances, it was a stroke of great good fortune that the precious documents fell into the right hands. Their value was recognised, and a selection from the diary was finally presented to the reading public in 1818.

It's easy to forget now what a landmark this was in English literature. The tradition of keeping a diary had only just begun in Evelyn's day, and there was nothing yet to rival this one. The fact that his entries were sometimes written in later, and that the volumes were therefore partly memoirs, does nothing to lessen the work's importance. It is still a first-hand record of the times, stretching right from his early years to within three weeks of his death at the age of 85, and chronicling not only a great stretch of family and local history, but also a series of truly sensational national events—the Civil War, the Restoration of the Monarchy, the Great Plague and the Great Fire of London.

Unfortunately, Evelyn is rather overshadowed now by that other great seventeenth-century diarist, Samuel Pepys. This is natural enough, for Pepys covered some of the same ground in a more intimate and revealing style. And this difference was natural, too, in view of their different circumstances, and attitudes towards diary-keeping. Evelyn had started life higher up the social scale, was about thirteen years older than Pepys, and had a large family (Pepys and his wife were childless). He took every aspect of his life more seriously. Instead of confessing his foibles and peccadilloes to his diary in shorthand code, he gave accounts of his days in closely-written but clearly decipherable longhand, and offered considered and often very critical opinions on society life. Gambling, drunkenness, bear-baiting and even French fashions in clothes all raise his hackles. He seems to have been reassuring himself, and any of his descendants who might see the entries, that he had spent his time profitably—not profligately.

Yet the two diarists, for all their contrasting backgrounds and person-alities, became fast friends, a sign in itself that there's much more to Evelyn than first meets the eye. In fact, in some important respects, this staunch and gifted Surrey gentleman has even more to offer than his younger, more fêted contemporary.

While Pepys was every inch a Londoner, Evelyn was a Surrey gentleman born and bred. "The Place of my birth was Wotton, in the Parish of Wotton or Black-Heath in the County of Surrey, the then Mansion house of my Father," he writes proudly. We must learn elsewhere that his paternal great-grandfather had come from Kingston, and his great-grandmother from nearby

Long Ditton, also that it was with the proceeds of gunpowder manufacture at Long Ditton that his grandfather had bought up Wotton and other Surrey estates for his sons. Evelyn focuses instead on the countryside into which he was born. He describes the house eloquently and accurately as a mansion

> sweetley environ'd with those delicious streames and venerable Woods, as in the judgement of strangers, as well as Englishmen, it may be compared to one of the most tempting and pleasant seates in the Nation ... For it has risings, meadows, Woods and Water in abundance ... Being but within little more than 20 miles from Lond: and yet so securely placed, as if it were an hundred.

He is proud too of his father's present eminence in the county, informing us that Richard Evelyn was the last High Sheriff of "Sussex and Surrey together" before the two offices became separate. In this capacity, he says later, his father was attended by 116 servants in green satin doublets, and "diverse Gentlemen and persons of quality besides," making well over three times as many staff as was usual for the position. There is no such retinue for High Sheriffs now, as more recent Evelyns can testify, some of them having been High Sheriffs in their turn. But they can content themselves with knowing that theirs is still the oldest secular office in the land, apart from the crown.

After praising his father's wisdom, calmness and modesty, Evelyn adds, "His estate was esteem'd to be about £4000 per an: well wodded, and full of Timber." By seventeenth-century standards, the family must have been extremely wealthy.

Today's "Church-porch of Wotton" where Evelyn "learnt his first lessons"

As well as inspiring him to create variegated views and leafy vistas himself, Evelyn's love of Surrey's trees, rivers and hills, is a recurrent theme throughout the diary. As a baby, either because it was customary in high-

24

class families or because his mother was weak (she would die while he was still at school), he was quickly put to a wet-nurse. He describes his wet-nurse like this—

> a neighbours wife and tennant; of a good comely, brown, and wholsome-complexion, and in a most sweete place towards the hills, flanked with wood, and refreshed with streames, the affection to which kind of solitude, I succked in with my very milke.

His spiritual and intellectual education kept pace with his education in nature, for he learnt his first lessons from "one Frier ... At the Church-porch of Wotton." Although he was soon sent away to his maternal grandparents in Lewes, Sussex, apparently because it was further from plague-ridden London, Wotton continued to shape his sensibilities. For instance, it was on one of his regular returns there, when he was about eleven, that the observant boy noticed his father keeping his records and decided to set down his own observations in a "blanke Almanack."

Since he was the second son of the family, Evelyn wouldn't inherit his father's estate until the death of his elder brother George in 1699, less than seven years before his own. Nevertheless, his roots would always be in "Wotton, the place of my birth." It was his base during his student days at Balliol College, Oxford, and at the Middle Temple in London, and he returned there frequently during his father's last illness (Evelyn was twenty then) and during his travels on the continent as a young man. He not only advised his brother on the gardens, but also worked on them himself, on one occasion writing with satisfaction about his design and construction of "a litle retiring place ... next the Meadow," where he had "made a triangular Pond or little stew, with an artificial rock." In the years to come, he would read and meditate here amid the beautiful scenes that he himself had done much to create.

We can see how close Evelyn was to his extended family in Surrey from the record of one of his homecomings. After George sent horses to fetch him from London, he spent a few days at Wotton "the place of my Birth, where ... I refresh'd my selfe and rejoyc'd," then went to stay with a cousin in Thames Ditton, then, after about three weeks in London, returned to Wotton again, making yet another visit to Wotton soon afterwards to see George's new baby son, after which he travelled immediately to Ewhurst, to visit his other brother Richard. A little later, we find him attending Richard's wedding in Epsom—and so on. On a slightly later visit from the continent, he makes particular mention of a delightful dip in his pool at Wotton: "return'ing to Wotton bath'd this Evening in the pond, after I had not for many years ben in cold Water."

Evelyn was already married by now. He had met and fallen in love with Mary Browne, the Royalist Ambassador's young daughter in Paris, and after returning to England for good in 1652 he brought her over (along with vast quantities of plant seeds and bulbs from France). The couple settled down to family life in Sayes Court, previously his father-in-law's estate at Deptford, then just inside Kent. All that remains of this estate, and the fabulous gardens which Evelyn laid out there, are a small nondescript park and a larger recreation area on either side of the A200 Evelyn Street, near the John Evelyn public house. The whole district has been completely absorbed into London now. Yet it was very close to Surrey's old county border then, and his connection with Wotton remained strong.

A pond on the Wotton House estate:
"I made a triangular Pond ... with an artificial rock"

This was helpful to Evelyn. He had only put in a brief appearance in the Civil War, but, as a dyed-in-the-wool Royalist, he'd been outraged when Charles I was beheaded, calling it an "execrable wickednesse," and he continued to keep a low profile during the rest of the Interregnum. Although he busied himself with improving his own estate, and cultivated his social life and artistic interests as well, he was always deeply grateful to his "hospitable" brother for making him welcome in the Surrey countryside.

The details of Evelyn's visits to friends and relations over the years bring seventeenth-century Surrey vividly to life. The roads, apparently, were no less dangerous then than now. After Richard's wedding, for instance, "the Coach in which the Bride and Bridegroome were, was over-turn'd in coming home." Luckily, notes Evelyn, no harm was done. As an older man, he could be as critical of new housing developments as people are now: "I went to Visite the Duke of Norfolck at his new Palace by Way bridge; where he has laied out in building neere 10000 pounds ... never in my daies had I seene such expense to so small purpose," he splutters. Or he could enthuse like any present-day sightseer over the beautiful bowers, copses and walks at Box Hill. And as he zealously attends weddings and funerals, stands as godfather to various babies (on one such occasion, noting particularly that he'd spent the grand sum of £18 on an inscribed plate), and visits sick friends, we may reflect that life in residential Surrey has changed very little in its essentials.

Evelyn's ties to Surrey came to the fore particularly in times of crisis. When his eldest child died in 1658, and the five-year-old's body was taken to nearby St Nicholas Church, Deptford, the distraught father yearned for it to be taken down instead to "Wotton c[h]urch in my deare native County Surry" so they could be buried together one day. The Evelyns lost two sons that terrible winter in Deptford, when crows' feet froze fast to their prey, and birds, fish and even people in their boats were frozen solid in the icy water of the Thames. Evelyn himself fell

John Evelyn's wife Mary,
as a young woman

seriously ill of a fever two years later, and was impatient to leave Deptford for his "Sweete and native aire at Wotton." And when disaster struck London with the Great Plague of 1665, he dispatched his pregnant wife and remaining sons to Wotton, even though he decided to stay at Sayes Court himself, to look after the Dutch prisoners-of-war then in his charge:

(1665) [September] 7 Came home, there perishing now neere tenthousand poore Creatures weekley: however, I went all along the

Citty and suburbs from Kent streete to St James's, a dismal passage and dangerous, to see so many Cofines exposd in the streetes and the streete thin of people, the shops shut up, and all in mournefull silence, as not knowing whose turne might be next: I went on to the D. of Albemarle for a Pest-ship, to wait on our infected men, who were not a few.

He was lucky to survive his contact with "multitudes of poore pestiferous creatures," and was rewarded with the safe birth of his first daughter Mary in Surrey, in the "same Chamber" in which he himself "had first tooke breath." Delighted with the news, he kept his family at Wotton for a further four months.

Evelyn's diary may be less spontaneous than Pepys's but his accounts of family and national crises are still riveting. These were the occasions when he was both passionately involved and morally and intellectually engaged. The struggle to accept the death of his first son—"he was all life, all prettinesse" cries the anguished father—and relinquish him to heaven, is heartbreaking, and the childless Pepys has nothing to offer of this intensity. Similarly, when the Great Fire breaks out, Evelyn's response is both heartfelt and practical.

(1666) [September] 3 God grant mine eyes may never behold the like, who now saw above ten thousand houses all in one flame, the noise and crakling and thunder of the impetuous flames, the shreeking of Women and children, the hurry of people, the fall of towers, houses and churches was like an hideous storme ...
    4 The stones of Paules flew like granados, the lead melting down the streetes in a streame, and the very pavements of them glowing with fiery rednesse, so as no horse nor man was able to tread on them ... nothing was like to put a stop, but the blowing up of so many houses, as might make a [wider] gap....

This disaster had made his own earlier tract against London's industrial pollution, *Fumifugium*, seem prophetic, and now, perhaps remembering the old family trade, he actively promoted the use of gunpowder to create spaces which the flames wouldn't be able to leap over. Later, the soles of his feet seared by the heat, his hair nearly singed, his breath taken away by the stench and the clouds of smoke, Evelyn clambered over the smouldering rubble to survey the damage in detail, and with incredible zeal presented his findings and proposals to Charles II within the week.

Evelyn's earnest desire to turn London from "the Suburbs of Hell" into a place where the air was "Serene and Pure"[3] and both people and vegetation could thrive (a place, in other words, more like his native Surrey), put him too far ahead of his time for his plans to be taken seriously. Yet he happened to have been to the old St Paul's a few days before the fire, in the company of

28

his good friend Christopher Wren and several others, and supported Wren's idea of rebuilding it with a "noble Cupola, a forme of church building, not as yet knowne in England, but of wonderfull grace." So at least one famous landmark in London may owe something to his continental taste.

Evelyn acted as godfather to one of Wren's sons, for the two men were close personal friends. This should come as no surprise. In addition to his many other talents, the diarist was an authority on architecture himself, having published his translation of Fréart de Chambrey's *Parallel of Ancient Architecture*, along with a treatise of his own on the subject, not long after *Sylva*. And although he heartily disliked the gambling and other vices at court after the Restoration in 1660, he was now at the height of his prestige and powers. Fascinated by the new advances in science, he had been a founder member of the Royal Society and was the translator and author of works on everything from the fine arts to politics and trade. The King himself had visited him at Sayes Court in 1663, and he numbered not only Wren but also the most influential men of every sphere among his friends.

Not least of these was the then Secretary of the Admiralty, Samuel Pepys. Evelyn was such a good friend of Pepys that he dined with him in prison when the younger man was at the Tower of London for "misdemeanours," and one of the jolliest passages in Pepys's diary is about Evelyn. The two were at supper with friends on 10 September 1665 (before Pepys's spell in the Tower), and Evelyn devised some witty verses so cleverly and quickly that he had them in fits of laughter—"in all my life I never met with so merry a two hours," wrote Pepys on his return home that night. Throughout this month, Evelyn's own diary entries concern the plague, the problem of feeding his Dutch prisoners-of-war, and his typically earnest and humane sympathy for the defeated Dutch Vice-Admiral. It's left to Pepys to reveal his friend's more fun-loving side.

That September had not passed without one of his regular visits to Wotton. In 1694, Evelyn, having remained close to his roots throughout his Deptford years, finally returned to them. There had been trouble over the lease of Sayes Court (he would not be able to pass it on to his heirs), and besides, the encroachments of the town and the problems of maintaining his gardens there had simply become too much for him. Evelyn also seems to have lost whatever influence he had had in the '80s, when he had been appointed a Commissioner of the Privy Seal. So when his brother offered the Evelyns an apartment at Wotton, they accepted:

(1694) May 4th. I went this day, with my Wife and 3 Servants from Says-Court, and removing much furniture of all sorts, books, Pictures, Hangings, bedding etc: to furnish the Appartment my Brother assign'd me; and now after more than 40 yeares, to spend the rest of my dayes with him at Wotton, where I was borne ... I pray God this solemn Remove may be to the Glory of his mercy, and the good of my family.

There the three elderly people lived together until George died in 1699 and left Evelyn in sole possession.

There are highlights even in these later years. Shortly after letting out Sayes Court, for instance, Evelyn can be seen laying the foundation stone of Greenwich Hospital with Wren. As treasurer of the project, he had been deeply involved with it from the start, as he had been earlier with the building of another famous London institution, the Royal Hospital at Chelsea.

Entwined E(velyn) and W(otton) on the front of Wotton House

But despite his homecoming to Surrey, and the deep feelings it obviously evoked, the last pages of the diary make gloomy reading. Added to the various ills of old age were the worries of keeping up Wotton House itself, and continuing concern about the fate of Sayes Court (in 1698 it was occupied by Peter the Great, who wrecked his famous holly-hedge, as gossip had it, by crashing into it in a wheelbarrow). Besides, there were the long-term prospects of Wotton to consider. The family was dwindling in front of Evelyn's very eyes. He had already lost all but two of his eight children, most recently his daughters Mary and Elizabeth, who had died of smallpox within six months of each other. The death of Mary, whose birth at Wotton he had greeted with such joy, had unleashed another great torrent of paternal grief in him (Elizabeth had died after an elopement, and his sorrow had seemed the less acute for it). Now he saw his last remaining son John succumb in middle age to "a tedious languishing sicknesse," and in the winter of the following year, 1700, Evelyn had a terrible fright:

[November] 5 Came the newes of my deare Grandsons (the onely male of my family remaining) being fall'n ill of the Small-pox at Oxford, which after the dire effects it had, taking a way two of my Children (Women grown) exceedingly Afflicted me."

Luckily, however, young Jack recovered, and, like any good Surrey gentleman, Evelyn then devoted himself single-mindedly to promoting his grandson's interests and protecting the future of the estate.

The end was soon to come. When Pepys died in 1703, Evelyn was already too frail to be a pallbearer: "my present Indisposition, hindred me from doing him this last Office." Appropriately enough, Evelyn's last diary entry, made three weeks before he died, consisted of notes from sermons. He died at the house in Dover Street, near Berkeley Square, which had belonged to his longest surviving son, John—his beloved grandson Jack's father—and from there his body was taken back to Wotton. He was laid to rest in the family chapel of the lovely old Saxon church of St John the Evangelist, on the other side of the A25 to Wotton House, where he had first learned his letters. His tomb, and various other memorials of the Evelyn family, can be seen there. However, the chapel has to be kept locked because of a bizarre incident of vandalism in 1992. The vandalism is a sad footnote to such an illustrious life, a comment on our age rather than anything to do with Evelyn himself.

"Wotton chur[c]h in my deare native County Surry"

It hardly matters. Evelyn's real and enduring memorials are his diary and the Surrey landscape.

As for the diary, had it been as dull as ditch-water, it wouldn't still be in print today. Fortunately, Evelyn had many good qualities as a diarist. Like Pepys, he did more than record family affairs or big historical events. Throughout his life he had an eye for curiosities. In his youth, we find him crawling to the very summit of Vesuvius, and stretching out full-length to peer into its crater, where he could make out "a hill shaped like a greate browne loafe ... continualy vomiting a foggy exhalation, and ejecting huge stones with an impetuous noise and roaring, like the report of many musquets discharging." In middle age, he marvels at a man at a Southwark fair who lifts up a piece of an iron cannon weighing 400lbs with his hair. And in his mid-sixties he observes in minute detail the first rhinoceros ever brought into England:

> (1684) [October] 22 Sir William Godolphin and I went to see the Rhinocerous (or Unicorne) ... That which was most particular and extraordinary, was the placing of her small Eyes in the very center of her cheekes and head, her Eares in her neck, and very much pointed ... but in my opinion nothing was so extravagant as the Skin of the beast, which hung downe on her haunches, both behind and before to her knees, loose like so much Coach leather...."

On another occasion, he and Pepys are to be found examining an infant prodigy together—they obviously shared a taste for the unusual.

Moreover, had it not been for the discovery of Evelyn's, then Pepys's diary might never even have seen the light of day. The Master of Magdalene College, Cambridge, was reading Evelyn's newly published diary, and he noted Evelyn's references to Pepys. His thoughts turned to six volumes in strange shorthand that were kept in the college's Pepys Library.... He dug them out and showed them to a relation of his, who began to understand what they were. And again, but with more effort to decode, a wonderful historical document was given to the world. This was another lucky find, like the original discovery of Evelyn's diary, without which we would have lacked two contemporary perspectives on a great swathe of our history, as well as the emergence of what many see as a unique literary form.

Evelyn's ability as a writer also helped to make *Sylva* and its supplement, *Kalendarium Hortense* (a gardener's almanac), best-sellers of their day. Both were landmarks in their own right. *Sylva* was the very first publication to have been officially sponsored by the Royal Society, while the *Kalendarium* was the only part of Evelyn's immense and elaborately annotated work-in-progress, *Elysium Britannicum*, to have found its way into print in his lifetime. The influence of the two manuals certainly accounts for some of Surrey's tree-splendour, in particular, perhaps, its extraordinary number of well-established Scots pines. Indeed, together with the fine examples of his own gardening at both Wotton and Sayes Court, these books helped to shape the whole future of gardening in England. Their author's enthusiasm, commitment, knowledge, and detailed diagrams paved the way for the great landscape gardens of the eighteenth century, and for the flood of garden manuals and gardening books of all types which have been published ever since. One particular fruit of Evelyn's endeavours was Kew Gardens in Surrey, of which his well-documented garden at Sayes Court, with all its curious horticultural species and innovations, was an important forerunner.

As for those innovations, some of Evelyn's advice and practices seem as fresh and relevant today as they were his own age. He advertised not only the benefits of planting trees, but also the need for getting birds into the garden, and keeping a good balance with useful insects. The elaborate glass-fronted beehive at Sayes Court, a gift from an Oxford don, was such a novelty that even the King came to look in on his busy bees. Distilling the essences of herbs and so on appeals to current taste as well, as does Evelyn's revolutionary practice (mentioned at the beginning of this chapter) of washing his hair with a "decoction" of some of these in warm water—something he started doing on 13 August 1653, in his early thirties. Even though he only did this once a year, it was a start, wasn't it?

Yet what I like most about Evelyn, even if it means that his diary isn't full of titillating little snippets like Pepys's, is his personality itself. The man who comes to such vivid life in his daily records is deeply reflective and pious, a solid pillar of the Church of England. Neither he nor, perhaps more significantly, the all-revealing and gossipy Pepys, has anything scurrilous to report about his behaviour. Questions are sometimes asked about Evelyn's attachment in middle age to one of the royal maids of honour, a young woman called Margaret Blagge, whom he described as "This Miracle of a young Lady in a licentious Court," and whose devotions he supervised. However, after her death he was a great support to her devastated widower, Sidney Godolphin, who repaid his concern by helping his grandson Jack secure a position at court. Godolphin even arranged a good marriage for the young man—to his own niece. If there was the merest hint of scandal in the relationship between Evelyn and his wife, it obviously never reached Godolphin's ears. Besides, no one could have examined Evelyn's feelings for this young woman more anxiously than he did himself. He left a record of this painful process, along with a biographical tribute to Margaret, and what it reveals more than anything else is the high-minded intensity and moral scrupulousness which pervaded all aspects of his life.[4]

By all accounts, Evelyn was a true Surrey gentleman, as sensitive as his portrait suggests, and as upright as a human being can be. A comment by Pepys about his "conceitedness," in the younger man's diary entry for 5 November 1665, is often taken out of context. Pepys is here talking primarily about Evelyn's rather touching pride in his efforts at plays and poetry. In other ways, Evelyn was evidently quite humble. Although he did accept an honorary doctorate from Oxford, he more than once turned down the offer of a knighthood, perhaps to emulate his own father, who had been "a studious decliner of Honors and Titles; being already in that esteeme with his Country, that they could have added little to him, besids their burthen." No doubt his refusal also had something to do with his dislike of the riotous court. At any rate, I think Pepys's later verdicts on his friend may stand: "a very ingenious man; and the more I know him the more I love him ... a worthy good man" (29 April 1666, 16 March 1669).

* * *

Naturally, a man like Evelyn who had such a wide social circle, can be linked with various other writers with Surrey connections.

Of these, the best known are probably the poet Abraham Cowley (1618–1667) and the dramatist John Vanbrugh (1664–1726). Evelyn encouraged Cowley, then living in retirement in Chertsey, to write an ode to the Royal Society: "Has Mr Cowley no inspirations for it? Would it not hang the most heroic wreath about his temples?" he wheedled, in a letter of 19 March 1667. The ode was duly composed, and is considered one of Cowley's finest works. As for the much younger Vanbrugh, who wrote *The Provok'd Wife* and other popular Restoration comedies, Evelyn successfully nominated him for the House of Lords in 1695. Vanbrugh was also an architect, as multi-talented in his own way as Evelyn was himself, and a few years after Evelyn's death he would build the original house at Claremont, in Esher.

Claremont in Victorian times

This house deserves a special mention here, as it will crop up again in later chapters. It would have an illustrious and sometimes sad history, passing through the hands of Clive of India (who rebuilt it on higher ground) and eventually going to Queen Victoria, who bought it for her beloved youngest son Leopold, Duke of Albany. It is now used by the Claremont Fan Court School on the A3 Portsmouth Road, and its beautiful gardens, landscaped in the eighteenth century by Capability Brown, belong to the National Trust. It's good to think of Evelyn furthering the career of someone who contributed such a special estate to this more northerly part of Surrey.

Finally, perhaps no one has written a more lively and moving introduction to Evelyn than Virginia Woolf, who herself spent some important years in Surrey, at Richmond, the original home of the Hogarth Press. Her essay on Evelyn first appeared as the leading article of the *Times Literary Supplement* of 28 October 1920. She isn't, of course, uncritical. She pictures Mrs Evelyn "cleaning ink stains from the carpets" while the great man is busy fulfilling his public duties. But, after all, as she reads the whole long story unfolded by the diary, she finds that "the spectacle of human life on such a scale is full of delight," and feels that "somehow or other the bygone gentleman sets up, through three centuries, a perceptible tingle of communication"—a "tingle" which we can still feel today, almost another century later.

Notes to Chapter 1

[1] This is Evelyn's description of it in "The Materials of Sallets," number 34 (on lettuce) in his fascinating *Acetaria: A Discourse of Sallets* (1699), available online at <www.gutenberg.org/etext/15517>, or from Prospect Books (Totnes, 1996). This isn't just a book about salads. Apart from giving food histories, information about cooking, and a great deal of advice to gardeners, Evelyn discusses vegetarianism at the end of his list of "materials," comparing it to the "blood and cruelty" involved in eating flesh, and insisting that it is possible to live "long and happily" on vegetables alone. Perhaps it was his own taste for olive oil (not "clogging" butter) and fresh vegetables that enabled him to live to such a good age himself.

[2] All quotations in this chapter are from *The Diary of John Evelyn*, selected and edited by John Bowle, Oxford: World's Classics, Oxford University Press, 1985, unless otherwise specified.

[3] Words from Evelyn's *Fumifugium: or the inconveniencie of the aer and smoak of London dissipated*, an extract from which is available at <www.cf.ac.uk/encap/skilton/nonfic/evelyn01.html>

[4] For a detailed and fair treatment of this intriguing episode, which tells us much about seventeenth century life, see Frances Harris's *John Evelyn and Margaret Godolphin: Transformations of Love*, Oxford: Oxford University Press, 2002.

Suggested Reading

1. From any available edition of the Diaries:
   Entries for 1658, in which Evelyn lost two sons, and witnessed a whale stranded in the Thames, and the funeral of Cromwell
   Entries for 1665, in which Evelyn observed wildfowl in St James's Park, ritual in the House of Lords, victory in the Dutch Wars—and The Plague
   Entries for The Great Fire of London, Sept. 2nd 1666 onwards
   Entries for early 1671, when Evelyn discovered Grinling Gibbons
   Entries for January 1684, about the Frost Fair on the Thames
2. Virginia Woolf's essay, "Rambling Round Evelyn," in *The Common Reader*, London: Hogarth Press, 1932. This is also available from Project Gutenberg on the web.
3. Francis Harris's *John Evelyn and Margaret Godolphin* (see note 4 above).

4. William Cobbett's account of the gardens at Albury, in his *Rural Rides*, Harmondsworth: Penguin, 1967, pp.98–100.
5. "Evelyn's and Pepys's Diaries Compared" (from *The Cambridge History of English and American Literature*) <www.bartleby.com/218/1003.html>

Places to Visit

Wotton House (tel. 01306 730000) is used for various public functions such as marriages, and so is open to non-residents. Its grounds can be viewed on request by asking at the main reception desk. It is shut during the Christmas and New Year period. The Wotton Hatch public house on the main road to the right of the driveway is a deservedly popular eating-place.

The Church of St John the Evangelist, where the Evelyns have a family chapel and various memorials, including coffin-shaped floor monuments to John and Mary Evelyn, is just over the road. Access to the chapel can be arranged by contacting The Rectory, Holmbury St. Mary, Dorking RH5 6NL (tel. 01306 730285). Members of the Vaughan Williams family are buried in the graveyard. Nearest station: Dorking. However, this whole beautiful part of the Surrey countryside is best visited by car.

Albury Park is about five miles away. The house as it stands now was designed by the famous Gothic Revival architect Augustus Pugin in the nineteenth century, and has 63 of his ornate and eye-catching chimneys. The little Saxon church there contains a memorial to Christopher Wren's mathematics tutor, William Oughtred, who was a rector of the church. The Evelyn Garden itself belongs to the estate of the Duke of Northumberland, and is only opened twice a year, once in March and once in October (contact the Surrey branch of the National Gardens Scheme, tel. 01483 222689). There is much of interest in the village itself, not only many other Pugin chimneys, but also Albury House opposite Albury Mill. Here lived Martin Tupper, a largely forgotten Victorian poet who had hoped for the Poet Laureateship which instead went to Tennyson. Newlands Corner just north on the A25 on the Albury Downs also has a famous literary association: it is the place where Agatha Christie mysteriously disappeared for eleven days in December 1926. There is a Countryside Centre there for tourists.

Claremont Landscape Gardens are on the A3 just past Esher. As National Trust property, they are regularly open to the public. The Claremont Fan Court School is occasionally open for guided tours, too (enquiries, tel. 01372 467841). Before going, it would be worth looking into a much later diary, that of Rev Francis Kilvert, who describes a visit there on 18 January 1871 in fascinating detail.

The John Evelyn pub in Deptford displays some interesting prints, including a facsimile of the end of Evelyn's will. Sayes Court Park, with its ancient mulberry tree (dating from around Evelyn's time), is just round the corner. At the back of nearby St Nicholas Church is the one Evelyn family memorial to have survived the London air raids, a wall plaque to his five-year-old son Richard and his nineteen-year-old daughter Mary (mentioning that Mary was born at Wotton). Also displayed are a model of Sayes Court, which includes even the eight walnut trees Evelyn planted to give shade to his milk herd, and a reredos panel near the altar, "The Valley of the Dry Bones," by Grinling Gibbons. Access can be arranged by telephoning the Deanery Administrator on 020 8692 8848. This church is also famous for its memorials both inside and outside to Christopher Marlowe, who died in Deptford and is buried here. Street names in this area recall Evelyn rather than Marlowe: Albury Street, Dorking Close, Abinger Grove, Larch Street and so on make one feel that Evelyn left a little bit of Surrey here. Nearest station, Deptford.

*The Geffrye Museum in Kingsland Rd, Shoreditch (tel. 020 7739 9893), open Tuesday–Saturday, 10am–5pm, and Sundays and Bank Holiday Mondays, 12–5 pm, has an ebony cabinet of Evelyn's at the back of the Stuart Room, with beautiful ivory inlays on the inside. Interestingly, the diary itself is said to have been kept in an ebony cabinet. This museum, housed in some old almshouses, is a fine place to get a sense of old English interiors, and has other attractions, such as a herb garden. Nearest tube station, Old Street.

2. Fanny Burney
(Madame d'Arblay) of Westhumble

Fanny Burney, 1752–1840

"Dear, ever dear Chesington," another diarist reminisces later in the eighteenth century, "wherat passed the scenes of greatest ease, gaiety, and native mirth that hath fallen to my lot."[1]

This diarist was Fanny Burney (1752–1840), who spent the happiest and most productive times of her life around ten miles from Wotton, in the area between Box Hill and Chessington. Her novels were admired in her own day by Dr Johnson and Jane Austen, and won her a permanent place in the history of English literature—a place acknowledged in our own age by the memorial window to her in Westminster Abbey's Poets' Corner. It was unveiled on 13 June 2002, the 250th anniversary of her birth.

38

To many, however, Fanny Burney's life story seems more colourful and dramatic than her fiction. So much so, that a Canadian academic, Joyce Hemlow of the Burney Papers Project, spent the best part of her career piecing it together from her journals and letters. When Professor Hemlow died in September 2001, she was given the unusual honour (for an academic) of a long obituary in the London *Times* of 8 November. This was a tribute both to her painstaking research, and the current popularity of her subject. Burney's star has never shone more brightly than it does now.

Unlike John Evelyn, Fanny Burney was born outside the county, having started life in King's Lynn, Norfolk, in 1752. But Surrey would soon become vitally important to her. She was only eight years old when her musician father decided to return to the City, where he'd already made a reputation for himself as a young man. He took his family with him. Sadly, his wife soon died of consumption after bearing their ninth child. Several earlier children had already died in infancy, and Charles Burney now feared for the remaining siblings. But help was at hand. His good friend, a failed playwright named Samuel Crisp, had found himself a retreat in the healthy Surrey countryside: Chesington Hall was a rambling and remote old house with panoramic views over the Epsom Downs, then being used as a kind of convalescent home. It soon became the Burneys' retreat as well.

Chesington Hall, where the young Fanny could write undisturbed.
Sketch by Ellen G. Hill

Young Fanny was nine when she first met Samuel Crisp, and he was 55. The middle-aged cynic teased and amused her, and she adored him. He called her Fannikins, and she called him "Daddy." They would be close friends until his death in 1783, when Charles (now Dr) Burney composed the lines which can still be seen on his memorial tablet at St Mary the Virgin's Church, Chessington, telling us that his friend's

> Good humoured wit and wide benevolence
> Cheered and enlightened all this hamlet round.

A tight community of cultured people developed in the area extending from Chesington Hall to Norbury Park near Box Hill. Norbury Park was another old estate, then owned by William Locke. Nothing now remains of Chesington Hall, which was rebuilt in 1803, but later pulled down to make way for a housing development. Only "Chessington Hall Gardens," a road near Chessington South station, gives a clue as to its location. Norbury Park, however, remains, and very grand it is too. When Susanna Burney, Fanny's younger sister, married a naval officer in 1782 and settled in nearby Mickleham, one of her three children was born unexpectedly early during a visit there, and she gave him the middle name of Norbury (by which name his aunt later liked to refer to him).

Norbury Park

Much of Fanny Burney's early work was written on visits to this area, where she had all the privacy and space she needed. First came *Evelina*, subtitled *The History of a Young Lady's Entrance into the World*, and published in 1778 when she was 26 (and Jane Austen was just three). The plot is typical of this author's work, and sounds dated enough: the heroine, an innocent and sensitive young woman very much like Burney herself, enters into society and, despite all kinds of hitches, captures the heart of a lord. Yet the writing still feels perfectly fresh today. Her heroine is spirited and observant, and her letters to her guardian in Dorset reveal not only her own embarrassments, but also the absurd ways of this new world in which she finds herself. Here is Evelina before her first ball:

I have just had my hair dressed. You can't think how oddly my head feels; full of powder and black pins, and a great cushion on the top of it. I believe you would hardly know me.... When I shall be able to make use of a comb for myself I cannot tell, for my hair is so much entangled, *frizled* they call it, that I fear it will be very difficult. (Letter X)

Worse discomforts soon follow, for Evelina disgraces herself at the ball by laughing at a particularly affected suitor, and is only rescued by the gallantry of Lord Orville—who, of course, is at once attracted to certain qualities in her, and will eventually make her his wife.

In one swoop, with this youthful first novel, Burney had given whole generations of women writers their subject-matter—girls on the brink of womanhood, their intimate thoughts and personal relationships, their ups and downs in society and the way they grow through being tested by it, and, last but by no means least, their search for true love. No wonder Jane Austen saw her as our first woman novelist.

Yet perhaps Fanny Burney's biggest gift to the future was purely practical. She showed that women could publish, be the talk of the town, and enhance rather than lose their good name. *Evelina* had come out anonymously at first, printed from a manuscript in disguised handwriting. Then everyone read it, including Dr Johnson and Sir Joshua Reynolds, who were family friends. Delighted that Dr Johnson, in particular, had admired it, Burney did a jig round the mulberry tree in the garden of Chesington Hall. "It is a *sweet* book," cooed Johnson's heartthrob, Mrs Thrale, going on to advise her: "the Book has such success—that if *you* don't own it—somebody else will!" So the cat was let out of the bag, and, as the sensational news of its (female!) authorship spread, the novel became even more popular, quickly going through four editions. George III's wife, Queen Charlotte, and the young princesses were among its many readers. Although later women novelists, from Austen to the Brontës and George Eliot, would still try to cloak their identities, here was the first step in granting them respectability.

Burney's success was particularly lucky for the author herself, because she had previously had to burn her creative writings—neither her father nor his new wife had thought it proper for women to air their views in public. It was only when her work was praised by people like Johnson, and such other members of their circle of friends as the philosopher Edmund Burke (who was said to have sat up all night reading it), that they could accept its propriety.

From this time until 1781, Fanny Burney was also a frequent guest at Streatham Park, the Surrey home of the Thrales, the very place where Mrs Thrale urged her to go public about *Evelina*. "Mr Thrale's House is white, and very pleasantly situated, in a fine Paddock," writes Burney, after her first dusty journey there in August 1778. There is still a Thrale Road in Streatham, linking a small common with the A216 Mitcham Lane close to the Surrey border, but it's very hard indeed to imagine that rural scene in urban Streatham now.

Here, the young author was much fêted, all the more so when she repeated her triumph with her second novel, *Cecilia*, in 1782. The first edition of 2,000 copies sold out in three months. It was so much the rage that even Napoleon read it.

Burney's new fame brought a quite unlooked-for result. The Queen took a keen interest in this bright new star in the literary world, and in 1786 offered her a position at court. Of course, it was a great honour. Burney thought that she would be able to further the prospects of her father and brothers, and besides, Dr Burney himself urged her to accept. Thus, pen poised to observe all the foibles and machinations of the court at first hand, she spent five years as one of the ladies-in-waiting, her official title being, "Second Keeper of the Robes."

Burney's duties were often performed at Kew Palace, so she continued to spend a good deal of her time in Surrey. And what a time it was! The setting itself was special enough. The palace, a vast redbrick mansion, and Queen Charlotte's Cottage, a separate small building with a more intimate and "olde worlde" feel, had been built so that the royal family could enjoy the recently established botanical gardens. Their fame had already spread. Only a few years before, William Cobbett, my next Surrey author, had run away from home to work there. For Burney, however, these beautiful surroundings were the scene of one of her most fraught encounters with the King, whose sanity was now in question:

> What was my terror to hear myself pursued!—to hear the voice of the king himself, loudly and hoarsely calling after me "Miss Burney! Miss Burney!—" I protest I was ready to die;—I knew not in what state he might be at the time.... Think, however, of my surprise, to feel him put both his Hands round my two shoulders, and then kiss my Cheek! .... He assured me he was quite well, as well as he had ever been in his life: and then enquired *how I did*, and *how I went on,* and whether I was *more comfortable?*

And so the interview continued, at a time when people weren't even supposed to enter the king's presence. It is much to Burney's credit that she treats the sensational meeting most sympathetically, and speaks gently of "the Royal Sufferer" in her letters and journals.

However, being a confidante of the royal family couldn't compensate for life in such a gilded cage. The "irksome and quick-returning labours of the Toilette" started early in the morning when she helped the Queen to dress, and ended at midnight, when she helped her to undress. At noon, too, the Queen would change into different clothes. Regal attire was very elaborate and the various stages of the process were time-consuming. The other court rituals were also trivial and boring to a creative mind, and Fanny was cruelly used by her immediate superior, to the point at which her health was undermined. Most of all, she missed her freedom, and felt "lost to all private

42

comfort, dead to all domestic endearment." When she slipped quietly out of the court one day to stand at the grave of her beloved "Daddy" Crisp, who had died in Chessington in 1783, she felt miserable indeed.

At last, Fanny Burney managed to escape the court altogether. In 1791, accepting reasons of ill-health, the Queen released her from service. After travelling round England for a while, she naturally gravitated towards Surrey again, where, as she explained to her eldest sister Esther, "I go to peace, good air, and the best and dearest society." For the next several years, all the most significant events of life took place there.

But it was no longer "Daddy" Crisp who was the great draw. The attraction now was one of the new residents over at Juniper Hall, at the edge of Norbury Park.

Juniper Hall, Box Hill, today

A plaque outside the Hall explains that this establishment, which had once been a coaching inn, "gave shelter in 1792 to a group of progressive French aristocrats who had fled to England to escape the worst excesses of the French Revolution." Monsieur d'Arblay, the tall, distinguished, exiled French General, the *aide de camp* of the Marquis de la Lafayette, impressed Burney from the start. She found not only his looks but also his openness

43

and poetic nature deeply appealing. The two were soon exchanging and correcting essays in each other's languages. By the time of Burney's 1793 visit, their relationship had already gone much further. On the last day of that March, she received an amusingly roundabout proposal from her admirer at Juniper Hall, in which he writes (in French), about his hope of getting some means of livelihood in England, making it clear that he wants to do so for her sake.

Alexandre D'Arblay

Their courtship was charming. Burney noted it all down meticulously, keeping every record of it, including their corrected "themes." She also spells out her qualms, her father's distress, and her friends' and relatives' opinions. The tale which emerges is both poignant and romantic, and we can see that the couple will be devoted to each other, as indeed they would be.

The path of true love never runs smooth. There were two main problems. Burney's was the age difference. She was 41 now, and he was 39. This tiny gap troubled her, even though the General looked older than his years. She wrote to her sister Susanna, who had now moved to Ireland,

I wish him a *younger Partner*. I do not wish myself richer—grander—more powerful, or higher born,—one of his first attractions with me is his superiority to all these considerations—no, I wish myself only to be younger." [2]

Susanna was the first to reassure her about this, as perhaps Fanny herself had expected. But Susanna took her up on the word "richer." This was her family's problem—how would dear Fanny manage to live with a penniless exile? Burney too worried about the £100 pension which she had been given for her services at court. Would it still be paid after her marriage, and even if it was, would it be enough to keep them going?

Nevertheless, Dr Burney gave his reluctant consent, and the marriage was planned. Fortune favours the brave. The pension from the Queen's Privy Purse continued, and the generous Lockes at Norbury Park offered to lease the couple a plot of land in their own grounds, facing Box Hill and overlooking the River Mole, for their future home. The marriage duly took place, though without the presence of Dr Burney, at the local church, St Michael and All Angels, Mickleham, with its lovely old Norman tower. It was solemnised again in the Sardinian Ambassador's private Catholic chapel in London, in order to avoid any problems later, should M. d'Arblay manage to recover his rights in France.

St Michael and All Angels, Mickleham

The young couple met their early struggles cheerfully. Unable as yet to build on their plot, they first took lodgings at nearby Phoenice Farm at the foot of Bagden Hill, then rented a cottage in the village of Great Bookham, less than three miles further north. Originally Pit Pound Cottage by the Fair Field, and referred to as L'Hermitage by Fanny, this is now the house actually called The Hermitage, just over the road to St Nicolas Church. To modern eyes, it looks quite big enough for a young couple, but later owners have added to it, and the original would surely have seemed cramped to people who were used to the great estates of friends like the Lockes. A blue-blooded French officer like M. d'Arblay would probably have found it particularly confining. Nevertheless, "the Country and Prospects are inviting," wrote Burney to a friend, and her husband soon set to with fork and spade, like any Englishman in charge of his first patch of earth. "[H]e works in the garden while I write," his new wife explained with some amusement,

> and he is drawing up a plan for it but this sort of work is totally new
> to him. Seeds are sowing in some parts where plants ought to be
> reaping and plants are running to seed while they are thought not

yet of maturity.... His greatest passion is for transplanting.... Roses take the place of Jessamines, Jessamines of honeysuckles and honeysuckles of lilacs, till they have all danced around as far as space allows.[3]

She also tells how he weeded away a whole asparagus bed, and pruned the hedge in true military style, with his sabre—but admits that his efforts did result in a full week's supply of cabbages for the table. Moreover, he succeeded in making some nice garden walks for them in the spring. To complete their rural idyll, the d'Arblays even kept a goat. And in 1794 there were two events which between them sealed their newlywed bliss. First, in March, Dr Burney was fully reconciled to the couple at last. Then, in December, forty-two-year-old Burney bore their only child Alexander, at what is even now quite an advanced age for a first pregnancy. He was baptised over the road at St Nicolas Church.

The Hermitage, Great Bookham, today

Burney had long been interested in drama, and while she was at court had started several tragedies. But the genre was more or less off-bounds to women in the eighteenth century, and, despite some evident talent for it, she had little more success than her beloved "Daddy" Crisp. Only one of her plays was performed on the London stage, and that only once, on 21 March 1795. It was withdrawn, ostensibly for changes to be made. Burney then settled down in her Surrey cottage to completing her third novel.

Camilla, perhaps the most appealing of her fictional works, was published by subscription in 1796. On the list of subscribers was a Miss J. Austen, this being the single occasion on which Jane Austen's name appeared in print during her own lifetime. It is clear, especially from *Sense and Sensibility* (which was started the following year), that the younger author was inspired by what she read. However, *Camilla* is worth reading for itself, not just for its influence on that one important reader. Indeed, it has certain fine qualities which wouldn't be found in her younger contemporary's work. For example, it has some delightful pictures of children, and intimate details of life inside the kind of country houses which Burney knew so well. Burney has her own delicate moral sense, too. There's a particularly endearing picture of the heroine cradling a poor woman's infant, and Camilla's sweet-natured sister Eugenia prefigures such child cripples of Victorian literature as Dickens's Tiny Tim, although she is taught quite unsentimentally by her father to confront the world with a strong nerve.

The novel did well, as it deserved to do. The money from it enabled the d'Arblays, at last, to carry out their building project. In this way, Fanny Burney, born forty years before Mary Wollstonecraft published her *Vindication of the Rights of Woman*, became the first woman writer in our literature to support her family by the pen.

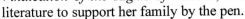

Camilla Cottage. Sketch by Ellen G. Hill

Although nature was not yet in vogue as a subject for lengthy descriptions, Burney did have an eye for it. An earlier journey from Streatham to Brighton with the Thrales had delighted her, especially when she "made out dear Chesington" in the distance. Now she enthused about the location of the proposed cottage. It would be built not on the plot originally offered, but on a field outside the park, so that one day (or so they hoped) it could be passed on to their son: "the situation of the field is remarkably beautiful," she reports to her father.

> It is in the valley, between Mr Locke's park and Dorking.... Imagine but the extacy of M. D'Arblay in framing All his own way an entire new Garden! He dreams now of Cabbage Walks— potatoe Beds—Bean perfumes and peas' blossoms. My Mother should send him a litle sketch to help his Flower Garden.

In 1797, it was ready. The d'Arblays called it Camilla Cottage, and moved into it with high hopes, having a picnic in one of the bare rooms, with some bread, boiled eggs and a gardening knife, before their furniture arrived. Little Alex galloped round the place using a stick as a make-believe horse, and all was excitement and triumph. Their own home at last, and in such beautiful surroundings, too!

However, this new rural idyll was comparatively short-lived. General d'Arblay couldn't devote himself indefinitely to defending his vegetables against rampaging farm animals and the Surrey frosts. As soon as it seemed safe to do so, he went back to France, at first only planning to visit family and friends. His wife quickly retreated to Norbury Park to have company while she awaited his return. But less than a month after his safe arrival, he was off again, and this time his wife and son followed. It was to be a ten-year stay, for the Treaty of Amiens in 1801 proved only a respite from the Revolution and the Napoleonic wars, and the family was still in France when war broke out again. When Burney finally returned to Camilla Cottage in 1812, their books and clothes were still intact, but the couple would never resume their life there. William Locke had died in 1810, and his son and heir proved less accommodating than his father. As in the case of John Evelyn and Sayes Court, the house couldn't be passed on after all. It was sold. In 1919, it would be burnt down, apparently still containing some of their possessions, including the General's "Letter Book." It was then replaced by a larger house called Camilla Lacey, since split into two separate properties (Camilla Lacey and Burney House) close to Camilla Drive.

The archway on which Fanny Burney's stay at Westhumble is commemorated

With not only "Daddy" Crisp but also her sister Susanna and the Lockes gone (Susanna had died in Ireland in 1800), Fanny Burney's attachment to Surrey waned.

Her life after leaving it was fraught with difficulties. Towards the end of her time in France, she underwent a mastectomy under the knife of Napoleon's surgeon, without any more anaesthetic than a glass of wine, and with nothing to cover her eyes but a fine cambric handkerchief—through which she could see far too much. This journal entry makes truly harrowing reading: "I refused to be held … Bright through the cambric I saw the glitter of polished Steel," and so on. As the *Times* doctor, Dr. Thomas Stuttaford, says in a piece on "The Power of Anaesthesia," coincidentally published on the very same day that Joyce Hemlow's obituary appeared, "Fanny Burney's description … makes the blood run cold." And she had barely recovered from this ordeal before she faced another: a dramatic and dangerous escape from France, via Dunkirk, on an American trading ship. It was her second attempt to get away, and even then she had to wait in Dunkirk for several weeks. She hated leaving her husband, but wanted particularly to remove their son from France in order to avoid his conscription into the French army. It would have been awful to have him forced to fight against her beloved England.

Her relief at having escaped was soon forgotten amid other worries. Her father was ailing, and for some time, Burney devoted herself to nursing him. He died in 1814, and she wrote a glowing tribute to him for his marble memorial tablet in Westminster Abbey, describing him as "The Pride Of His Family, The Delight Of Society, The Unrivalled Chief, And Scientifick Historian, Of His Tuneful Art!" That was also the year in which her fourth and last novel, *The Wanderer*, was published. She had brought it over with her from France with great care, but it wasn't a success, and from then on she gave up writing fiction.

Worse was to follow. Leaving Alexander to complete his education at Cambridge, she returned to her husband, only to become involved in the flight of the Royalists when Napoleon returned from Elba in 1815. She saw and recorded the terror and confusion after the Battle of Waterloo in such journalistic detail, and captured the atmosphere so well, that Thackeray is said to have drawn on the account for his own description of it in *Vanity Fair*:

> It is not near the scene of Battle that War, even with Victory, wears an aspect of Felicity! no, not even in the midst of its highest resplendence of Glory. A more terrific or afflicting sojourn than that of Brussels at this period can hardly be imagined…. Maimed, wounded, bleeding, mutilated, tortured victims of this exterminating contest, passed by every minute:—the fainting, the sick, the dying & the Dead, on Brancards, in Carts, in Waggons, succeeded one another without intermission….[4]

In the October of that year, she brought her lamed husband back to England, where, despite all attempts to nurse him back to health at their lodgings in Bath, he finally died in 1818.

Burney was to live another twenty-two years. Much of that time she devoted to writing a memoir of her father, a project which also had limited success. She was unlucky, too, in her beloved son. He had been a worry and a disappointment to her, and just when he seemed to be settling down at last, he died suddenly of influenza, under rather strange circumstances (he refused to let his mother enter the sickroom, giving rise to speculation that he may have had syphilis). She lived only three more years, dying in London in 1840. Despite all the stirring events of her life, she had reached the ripe old age of 87, and seen in the Victorian age. She was buried beside her husband and son, in Wolcot churchyard in Bath. Later in that century, the family's connection with Surrey was resumed: in 1870, Charles Burney, a nephew's son, became Vicar of St Mark's Church on Church Hill Road, Surbiton. From 1879 he was also Archdeacon of Kingston. He died in 1905 and is buried in the churchyard there.

***

Only one point about Fanny Burney's Surrey years remains, but it's an intriguing one. Jane Austen's brother famously said, "It is probable that she never was in company with any contemporary authors."[5] Yet there is at least a possibility that Jane Austen did meet the older novelist, and even based one or more of her characters on her. The question then is, *which* one?

The d'Arblays' friends and neighbours in Great Bookham were the Reverend Samuel Cooke, who had baptised baby Alex in 1795, and his wife Cassandra. As Austen's biographers invariably note, Cassandra Cooke was a cousin of Mrs Austen, and the Reverend Cooke had been chosen as Jane Austen's godfather. Mrs Austen duly brought her daughter to stay at the Rectory at least twice. A visit was definitely projected in 1799, within two years of Fanny's move to Camilla Cottage, when Fanny was still on "dropping in" terms with the Cookes. It seems likely that Jane (who was about 24 then) would have been introduced to local society while she was there, and it would be strange if the d'Arblays had not been included— especially since Jane herself had subscribed to *Camilla* only three years before.

True, there is no particular reference in Fanny Burney's letters to meeting the Cookes' guests, but such a meeting wouldn't have been of any importance to her. She would have known nothing of young Miss Austen's secret talents at that time, or for years afterwards. How about Jane Austen's letters, then? Although the plan to visit Bookham comes up in a letter of 11 June 1799, and nothing happened to prevent her from going, no letters exist from the visit. This in itself is significant, for they were apparently destroyed by her sister, whose eagerness to protect her reputation resulted in a number of such "deletions." Letters from this time may well have contained some critical comments about the Cookes themselves. Jane had not been looking forward to the visit. According to David Nokes, one of her most recent and thorough biographers, this was precisely because "Mrs Cooke was always

50

going on about her great friend and neighbour Madame D'Arblay," besides which, Mrs Cooke had just had some success herself with her historical novel *Battleridge*, which "did nothing to endear her to an aspiring literary rival."[6] But there might also have been some unacceptable references to Mrs Cooke's more celebrated friend. Professor Nokes himself writes later that Jane and her sister "had always liked to laugh at the way that literary people talked, especially the Cookes' Bookham friends, the Burneys, with their *'caro sposo's*." The two sisters are unlikely to have known how the "Burneys" talked to each other if they had never met them.

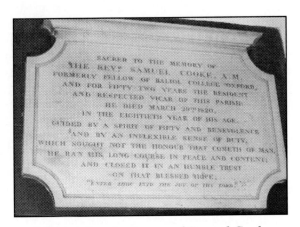

Memorial to the Reverend Samuel Cooke
in St Nicolas Church, Great Bookham

It is all very speculative, but there are two characters in the younger novelist's work who might owe something to a first-hand encounter with Fanny Burney. One is the pretentious Mrs Elton in her "Surrey" novel, *Emma*, who also calls her husband *"caro sposo,"* and gushes about grand houses, music and the Surrey countryside—"It is the garden of England, you know. Surry is the garden of England," she repeats smugly in Chapter 32. The other is Fanny's namesake, the sensitive Fanny Price of *Mansfield Park*. While Mrs Elton would have been rather a mean caricature, this heroine would have been a very sympathetic portrait indeed. Yet there's no need to chose between the two versions. The caricature may have represented Jane Austen's instinctive recoil from the flourishes of an older woman with courtly ways and a continental husband, while the later portrait may have represented Jane Austen's more mature insight into a woman of real sensibility.[7]

For, however Jane Austen felt if she ever did meet Fanny Burney face to face, there's no doubt at all that she had the highest respect for her quality of mind as a fellow-writer. "Oh, it is only a novel," she writes in Chapter 5 of *Northanger Abbey*:

It is only *Cecilia* ... Or, in short, only some work in which the most thorough knowledge of human nature, the happiest delineation of its vanities, the liveliest effusions of wit and humour are conveyed to the world in the best chosen language.

Putting something of Fanny Burney into a heroine with hidden depths like Fanny Price would have been another way of paying generous tribute to *Cecilia*'s author.

What is clear, at any rate, and agreed upon by all sides, is that Burney was a pioneering novelist with a fresh, vigorous and humane voice. She balanced an acute sensibility with humour and good sense, and in so doing set new parameters for women's fiction. Her legacy was huge, and she deserves the recognition that she is getting now. It's pleasant to think that her gifts found their full expression during the happiest days of her life, in her beloved Surrey. And it's fun, just as a footnote, to imagine Jane Austen staying in Fanny Burney's old neighbourhood in Great Bookham, and even, perhaps, having some contact with her distinguished literary predecessor.

Notes to Chapter 2

[1] Quoted by Annie Raine Ellis, editor, *The Early Diary of Fanny Burney, 1768–1778*, London: Bell, 1913, pp.lvii–viii. Other quotations from Burney, unless specified below, are from *Frances Burney: Journals and Letters*, selected by Peter Sabor and Lars E. Troide, Harmondsworth: Penguin Classics, 2001.

[2] *The Journals and Letters of Fanny Burney, Vol. 2, Courtship and Marriage 1793*, edited by Joyce Hemlow and Althea Douglas, Oxford: Clarendon, 1972, p.41.

[3] Quoted by S.E.D. Fortescue, *People and Places: Great and Little Bookham*, Great Bookham: Fortescue, 1978, p.50.

[4] *Fanny Burney: Selected Letters and Journals*, edited by Joyce Hemlow, Oxford University Press, 1987. Incidentally, Thackeray himself made some forays into Surrey during the writing of *Vanity Fair*, and is particularly remembered in Surbiton.

[5] Quoted, for example, by another novelist, Carol Shields, in *Jane Austen*, London: Weidenfeld & Nicolson, 2001, p.118.

[6] *Jane Austen: A Life*, London: Fourth Estate, 1997, p.193.

[7] Note that Pat Rogers also discusses the connection between Burney, the Cookes and the Austens in the *Times Literary Supplement* of 23 August 1996. He fails to mention Austen's 1799 visit though, concluding that she could only have known Burney at second hand. Yet he too sees Burney in Fanny Price. Would Jane Austen really have understood Burney so well simply by gossiping, as Rogers suggests—particularly with the Cookes' younger children, whom Burney disliked? I wonder!

Suggested Reading

1. Selections from the Penguin *Frances Burney: Journals and Letters*, edited by Peter Sabor and Lars E. Troide (see note 1 above):
   A humorous account of daily life at Chessington, pp.69–70
   Last visits to the dying Dr Johnson, pp.204–9 (NB Johnson's words about Mrs Thrale refer to her recent remarriage, which was considered highly unsuitable.)
   Encounter with the King in Kew Gardens, pp.280–5
   Letter to her friend Georgiana from Phoenice Farm, revealing her marriage, pp.366–9
   A humorous account of the French style of greeting, pp.424–5
2. Fanny Burney's *Camilla: Or a Picture of Youth* (Oxford World's Classics, 1999).
3. Kate Chisholm's *Fanny Burney: Her Life, 1752–1840* (Chatto & Windus, 1998).
4. Hester Davenport's *Faithful Handmaid: Fanny Burney at the Court of King George III* (Sutton, paperback, 2003).
5. For a brief introduction online, see the *Cambridge History of English and American Literature*, Vol. X <www.bartelby.com/220/1111.html>

Places to Visit

The memorial to Samuel Crisp is in St Mary the Virgin Church of England Church, Chessington, near Chessington South Station. It is a large marble plaque on the north wall towards the west end. Contact the vicarage (tel. 020 8397 3016) for access details.

Watercolour at Juniper Hall, possibly by General D'Arblay

Juniper Hall (tel. 0845 458 9219), is still there on Headley Lane, just off the Old London Road (B2209). The building is owned by the National Trust, but leased out as a Field Studies Centre which runs day and residential courses on insect photography etc. There is a very appealing water-colour picture of the Hall and gardens inside, which is thought to be by d'Arblay himself. Dated 1800, it manages to be both courtly and lively at the same time, showing people of all ages enjoying themselves in the garden, along with their dogs. Deer and sheep can be seen in the foreground. D'Arblay was fond of all the components of this scene, and it certainly seems likely that he was the artist.

Norbury Park, the Lockes' imposing house, can be glimpsed from the road here, from a distance, surrounded by trees. It was later the home of Marie Stopes, the pioneer of birth control. The house is privately owned, but most of its land now belongs to Surrey County Council. It is very popular with walkers, and has a marked cycle route. The best-loved area is the "Druids Grove," with its famous old yew trees. A walk around here is described by David Weller in his *Riverside Walks*, Newbury: Countryside, 1999, p.40.

St Michael's Church, Mickleham, where Fanny was married, is on a corner of The Old London Road just a little further north. (Notice the texts on grave boards there—an old feature of Surrey graveyards. There is also an imposing grave and plaque here to a former prime minister of Canada.)

The Hermitage, the more recent name of the house at Great Bookham which the d'Arblays rented, and where Fanny had her first and only child, is on Lower Road opposite St Nicolas church. It is privately owned. Interestingly, Fanny would refer to their next home, Camilla Cottage, as "our little Hermitage" as well.

The Church of St Nicolas, where the d'Arblays' baby was baptised, also has a plaque to the Rev. Samuel Cooke, their friend and Jane Austen's godfather. (See also Chapter 4 below). Note that although Bookham is on the main railway line to Waterloo, there is no train service on Sundays.

The plaque commemorating the d'Arblays' stay in Camilla Cottage is on the archway to the left of Westhumble & Boxhill Station, which is now a very small halt, but has an hourly service to Victoria.

Kew Palace and Queen Charlotte's Cottage are in the Royal Botanic Gardens at Kew (tel. 020 8332 5655). The palace has now re-opened after restoration. Entry to Queen Charlotte's Cottage is included in the admission charge of the Gardens, but opening times are limited. However, it can always be enjoyed from the outside, preferably in May, in the bluebell season!

*The Fanny Burney window in Poet's Corner is in the south transept of Westminster Abbey. Dr Burney's memorial, bearing Fanny's long encomium to him, is to be found in the third bay of the north choir aisle.

3. Country Writers in Surrey:
William Cobbett and Richard Jefferies

Both John Evelyn and Fanny Burney loved the Surrey countryside. They lived in it for long periods, and enjoyed it as a backdrop to their own activities, the "scene" of significant events in their lives—whether birth, marriage or the birth of their children. The countryside represented another way of life for them, away from the hustle and bustle of the metropolis, but the distinction wasn't as complete as it might have been. Evelyn worked hard to make another bit of Surrey in Deptford, and for a long time succeeded, while Burney gathered a group of sophisticates round her in the Box Hill area, much as she would have done in town. Perhaps neither would have been content without this degree of overlap. As for the natural world, there was nothing sacrosanct about it. Evelyn thoroughly changed the lie of the land in Wotton and at Albury, and imported plant life of all kinds from other parts of the country, and from abroad; while Fanny smiled to see her husband moving bushes around and hacking away at hedges just as energetically, but on a smaller scale.

Surrey's "Country Writers" are a different breed altogether, and one which would only emerge as England changed from a predominantly rural, agricultural nation to an urban, industrial one. Then indeed the countryside became precious, special, something to be preserved at all costs (Evelyn was already beginning to feel this at Sayes Court, right on the edge of London). The typical modern nostalgia for the old rural life was born, as was the romantic appreciation of wild nature, and with it, Romanticism itself. New ways of writing about the countryside were bound to follow.

Two writers who focused on the countryside are William Cobbett (1763–1835) and Richard Jefferies (1848–87). Cobbett was a Surrey author born and bred, whose *Rural Rides* was first published in instalments from 1822–26, while Richard Jefferies was a Wiltshire man, who, however, only became well known when he moved to the Kingston area in 1877.

Both were keen nature-lovers, who loved to be outdoors, and recorded their observations in their journalism. Yet they could not have been more different in character or purpose.

Cobbett, a farmer at heart, was a robust, practical and adventurous person who rode through the English countryside, particularly the southern counties, to gather information for political and economic reform. He was bursting with energy, both mental and physical. As well as being a commentator on rural England, he was a journalist and parliamentarian. In fact, all three roles were interrelated. He hated to see the fabric of the old agricultural communities being torn apart, and made it his mission to speak up for the rural poor. In so doing, he earned himself the nickname of "The Poor Man's Champion." To many, then, Cobbett is less a literary figure than a political one. Perhaps he is best known now as the original name behind Hansard, the long-running official record of parliamentary debates: Hansard was the name of the printer to whom he sold his *Weekly Political Register*, where *Rural Rides* first appeared.

Jefferies too expressed sympathy with the poor. "That any human being should dare to apply to another the epithet 'pauper' is, to me, the greatest, the vilest, the most unpardonable crime that could be committed," he wrote in Chapter 10 of his autobiographical book, *The Story of My Heart*. But he had no particular fondness for the farm labourer, and wasn't a campaigner. Rather, he was an introvert who was unwilling to engage with the contemporary (Victorian) world:

> I want to be always in company with these, with earth, and sun, and sea, and stars by night. The pettiness of house-life—chairs and tables—and the pettiness of observances, the petty necessity of useless labour, useless because productive of nothing, chafe me the year through. I want to be always in company with the sun, and sea, and earth. These, and the stars by night, are my natural companions. (*The Story of My Heart*, Chapter 7)

And although he too yearned to be physically robust, he was increasingly dogged by ill-health, and became more spiritual than spirited—a mystic, and, to many, a prophet. His longing to be at one with nature strikes a chord with modern readers, and he has a cult following even today.

Cobbett's birthplace: The William Cobbett, Farnham.
Watercolour by Janet Gale

William Cobbett

William Cobbett, 1763–1835

Cobbett was born in Farnham, in the south-west of Surrey, in 1763. About forty years before, Daniel Defoe had described the place as:

> a large populous market-town … and without exception the greatest corn-market in England, London excepted; that is to say, particularly for wheat, of which so vast a quantity is brought every market-day to this market, that a gentleman told me, he once counted on a market-day eleven-hundred teams of horse, all drawing waggons or carts, loaden with wheat….[1]

In the midst of this thriving centre of the old agricultural economy, Cobbett's father himself grew crops and kept an inn which came to be called The Jolly Farmer. It is still there on Bridge Square by a pretty stretch of the River Wey, and has a plaque commemorating the author/parliamentarian's birth. It was renamed The William Cobbett in the 1970s.

A few decades earlier, Arthur Mee, the compiler of the King's England Series, a county by county guide to England's treasures, had described Cobbett as Farnham's "greatest son."[2] Little has changed since then. The garden of the Museum of Farnham in West Street has a fine bust of the writer, looking as solid and determined as (according to William Hazlitt, in his essay on Cobbett in *The Spirit of the Age*) he looked in life, and an upstairs room displays various memorabilia, including Cobbett's spectacles, the inkwell which he used in Newgate prison while imprisoned for "sedition" (actually, for denouncing harsh measures to suppress a mutiny of the Ely militia), his seal, a candle-holder and pen stand from "the Female Reformers," a silver cup presented to him for reducing turnpike tolls, and so on.

The William Cobbett Society has prepared a Cobbett trail round Farnham, which takes visitors to various spots associated with him, and helpful study notes are also available in the museum: "William Cobbett 1763–1835: The Poor Man's Friend." It's even possible, once a year, to follow one of Cobbett's "Rural Rides" by coach. As the poet Edward Thomas said of the Farnham area early in the twentieth century, "There is no doubt about Cobbett's country."[3]

Cobbett came from good yeoman stock. His grandfather as well as his father worked the land. No wonder Cobbett had so much sympathy for the rural poor. He himself grew up with his three brothers, helping in the fields and playing by the river, and staying sometimes with "dear, good old grandmother Cobbett."[4] His father taught him how to read and write, and the basics of arithmetic, but it was primarily an open-air childhood, something for which he was later profoundly grateful.

He certainly learnt how to stand up against injustice. Once, having been whipped by a huntsman for going to the rescue of the hare, he retaliated by leading the next hunt into a bog, laying a false trail for the hounds with a red herring. Red herrings were traditionally used to train hounds, a technique that must lie behind the idiomatic use of "red herring" to refer to a false clue. With incidents like this to recall, no wonder Cobbett was glad not to have been "brought up a milk-sop, with a nursery-maid everlastingly at my heels."

Like any country boy at that time, Cobbett was soon set to work scaring birds, weeding, hoeing the earth, and so on, but he was no ordinary country boy, and wouldn't be content with an ordinary life. The first sign of this came when he was fourteen, and earning his living by working in the grounds of Farnham's picturesque Norman Castle. This was when he heard of the wonders of Kew. Determined to see the new royal gardens for himself, he set out the next day, walking the length of the county to reach them, and got a job there as a gardener's boy. (As mentioned earlier, this was before Fanny Burney began to visit Kew in the Queen's service.) The episode ended when his father arrived to fetch him home, but it had been a pivotal experience, not just because of what he learned about plant management, but because on the last leg of his journey to Kew he had bought a copy of Jonathan Swift's satirical *Tale of the Tub*.[5] This marked the beginning of a true autodidact's education, which was helped by later employment with an erudite vicar, and, after he had enlisted in the army at the age of twenty, by his work as a regimental clerk. The army took Cobbett to New Brunswick in Canada, and it wasn't until the end of 1800 that he finally settled in England again.

The gardens of Farnham Castle, where Cobbett worked as a boy

The events during the colourful intervening years would fill a book on their own. He married, fled to America to avoid an unfair court martial, taught English to French immigrants there and wrote a grammar book for them, and, perhaps most important of all for his future career, established himself in exile as "Peter Porcupine." Peter Porcupine was the pen-name of a very prickly-quilled English pamphleteer and columnist who denounced the republican enemies of the King, and anyone else who contravened his own ideas of justice and common-sense. The Surrey lad, whose rustic clothes had once amused the young English princes at Kew, had come a long way.

Even after his return to England in 1800, Cobbett's self-appointed role as an outspoken political commentator and reformist guaranteed a chequered life. At first, all seemed to be going well. The success of his *Weekly Register* enabled him to buy a farm in Hampshire, Surrey's south-western neighbour, and he settled down there with his wife to raise a family of seven children. But his spell in Newgate between 1810 and 1812 was a disaster for his finances. It was followed by a second prison term, for debt, in 1816. His radical opinions led to another period of exile in America, as well. The farm had to be sold, and exchanged for a smallholding in Kensington, which he ran as a seed-farm and plant nursery, more as a hobby than for its contribution to his livelihood. It was from here, on the site now partially occupied by Kensington High Street tube station, that he set off on his "Rural Rides," perhaps partly to escape what he called "the great Wen" (a term which vividly shows his disgust with the way London was spreading, and feeding off the rest of the country).

Nothing could have suited such a man more than this ambitious and demanding fact-finding mission. It challenged him physically, which he enjoyed, and brought him into contact with the soil and landscapes that he loved. In addition, it gave him ample opportunity to rail against the treatment of the rural poor, and to extol the last vestiges of traditional English life which he found in the small communities he visited. The result was a vibrant, entertaining travel book, one of the best in the language, always informed by his own extrovert, opinionated, larger-than-life personality.

Cobbett never made the rides easy for himself. He scorned to do so. On one long journey, for example, he was so outraged by having to pay road tolls that he fasted, rather than buy food on the way: "I was resolved, that the country, in which these tolls were extorted, should have not a farthing of my money." This was a matter of principle, not a sign of meanness. When he did eat, he would set aside whatever he could, either of the food itself, or of the money saved in not ordering more, for the poor: "I know well, *that I am the better* for not stuffing and blowing myself out, and with the savings I make many and many a happy boy." Neither bad weather nor reports of difficult roads deterred him. A thorough soaking by heavy rain was once seen as a "remedy" for the whooping cough that had been plaguing him for months. As for roads, he wrote triumphantly of one late November journey,

> Those who had so strenuously dwelt on the dirt and dangers of this route, had said not a word about the beauties, the matchless beauties of the scenery.... I must leave to imagination what it is, when the trees and hangers and hedges are in leaf, the corn waving, and the hops upon the poles!

A moment later, with the wry comment that "Men ... are not to have such beautiful views as this without some *trouble*," he has to dismount from his struggling horse, and slither down a slope by "taking hold of the branches of the underwood."

This dauntless explorer is both extremely knowledgeable about the countryside he sees, and extremely protective.

As for knowledge, he is a worthy successor of the pioneering Hampshire naturalist Gilbert White, whose *Natural History and Antiquities of Selborne* had been published in 1788. But he is also a pioneer himself—for, as a journalist, he is the father of modern columnists like Derwent May, whose daily "Nature Notes" in the *Times* keep us in touch with the countryside. Here is Cobbett, for example, helpfully distinguishing between two similar breeds of bird by their behaviour:

Quails assemble in flocks like larks, starlings or rooks. Partridges keep in distinct coveys; that is to say, the brood lives distinct from all other broods until the ensuing spring, when it forms itself into pairs and separates.

The soil is of particular interest to him, and he knows what grows well in it. Of the Weald of Surrey, he says, "the land is a stiff tenacious loam at top with blue and yellow clay beneath." Then he adds, "Here the oak grows finer than in any part of England. The trees are more spiral in their form. They grow much faster than upon any other land." Every detail here can be trusted. Old English "wald" meant "wooded upland," and oaks grow more prolifically in the Weald's clay mix than they do in any other English county (the Surrey coat of arms carries an oak sprig bearing an acorn). Moreover, these oaks are indeed considered spiral in form—which is unfortunate, because such oaks are especially prone to the modern disease causing "Sudden Oak Death."

Of course, Cobbett's fund of knowledge was particularly valuable to farmers. He published three books in the very year (1822) in which the *Rural Rides* began: *Cottage Economy, The Farmer's Friend,* and *The Farmer's Wife's Friend.* On the rides, he takes the opportunity to see what is actually being done in the countryside. Hops are of great interest to him, since his native Farnham was a centre for them in those days, but he offers his expert opinion on many other crops. Eyeing a field of turnips just outside Farnham, for instance, he points out what is wrong with the planting of it, and says disapprovingly, "I have no scruple to assert, that if it had been sown after my manner, it would have been a crop, double the weight of that which it now will have." We need not doubt that he was right. Although the agricultural sector was shrinking and becoming more mechanised, *Cottage Economy* went into many editions during the next hundred years or so, and indeed is still in print today.

However, there was a limit to how much the common man could improve his own lot, and Cobbett knew it. He could hardly contain his rage at the way local labourers and craftsmen were being squeezed by the "tax-eaters and monopolisers in the Wen," not to mention profiteering middlemen and harsh landlords. He wrings his hands over the results—the dwindling of such local industries as blanket-making in the Cotswolds, or the poverty of farmers around Salisbury, who get no benefit from their own rich produce. Not only machinery and monopolies, but also the large-scale enclosure of common land, the replacement of the solid old farmhouses with "mere painted shells" of newer dwellings, and empty churches in depopulated villages—all these and many more ignite his wrath. One of the diatribes in his second rural ride is sparked off by the mills on the Tillingbourne at Chilworth, close to Evelyn's Wotton, an area which he particularly loved and admired:

This valley, which seems to have been created by a bountiful providence ... has been, by ungrateful man, so perverted as to make it instrumental in effecting two of the most damnable of purposes ... namely, the making of *gunpowder* and of *bank-notes*! Here, in this tranquil spot, where the nightingales are to be heard earlier and later in the year than in any other part of England; where the first bursting of the buds is seen in Spring ... here has the devil fixed on as one of the seats of his grand manufactory; and perverse and ungrateful man not only lends him his aid, but lends it cheerfully!

The valley of the Tillingbourne, "which seems to have been created by a bountiful providence"

As often as not, a rant like this swells into an attack on the whole establishment, which he calls contemptuously the "Thing." But if he can name and shame an individual, a cruel landlord for instance, or a "hanging judge," he does so. And in doing so, Cobbett lays the foundation not only for many nineteenth-century reforms, but also for a whole breed of British columnists who "say it like it is," even at risk of libel charges. Another column in the *Times* comes to mind. It carries the by-line, "The Thunderer." Outspoken and fearless columnists are essential to free speech in a democracy.

Soon after *Rural Rides* appeared in book form, Cobbett had his greatest triumph. He was again taken to court, this time on a charge of inciting riots among the farmworkers with an article entitled "Rural War." He conducted his own defence, calling the top people in the government, including the Prime Minister himself, as his witnesses—and was rewarded with an acquittal. This should have helped to offset his bitterness about his earlier imprisonments. However, he had been through so much by now that it only made him, if anything, even more belligerent.

Although Cobbett went on to become a Member of Parliament for Oldham in Lancashire, he returned to Surrey again for his last years, leasing Normandy Farm in Ash, a village just outside Farnham—the town which he had described nostalgically in the General Preface to his *Journal of a Year's Residence in the United States* as "the neatest in England, and I believe, in the whole world." Sadly, there were still money problems, and he was now so stubborn and hard to get along with that he lived separately from the rest of his family. So this wasn't at all the Indian summer that it might have been. Nevertheless, he died in June 1835 with his wife by his bedside, and his ideals unshaken. His last speech in Parliament, in the previous month, had been in support of the rural poor, and his last trip outdoors, just the day before his death, had been to check that the farm was in good order. He was buried in St Andrew's Parish Church, Farnham, beside his forbears, and thousands of simple country folk flocked to join MPs and other notable figures in paying their last respects to him.

Cobbett memorial in St Andrew's Church, Farnham

Farnham is right to be proud of its famous "son." For all Cobbett's pugnaciousness (or perhaps because of it), his life had been a good and useful one. He had packed a tremendous amount into it. *Rural Rides* was only one of his many books, which include everything from gardening manuals to a history of the Protestant Reformation, and an English Grammar only recently reissued in the Oxford Language Classics series. Always keen to practise what he preached, he had even opened a long treatise on corn on paper actually made from environmentally-friendly cornhusks. He had stood up for the disadvantaged, often to good effect; set an example to modern politicians and political commentators; and strengthened the resolve to keep local crafts alive and save our countryside from over-development. One biographer, George Spater, writes in the Epilogue to his two-volume account of him, "Trees were grown, crops were cultivated, lives were shaped, by Cobbett's enthusiasms." Surrey, still such a beautiful county despite its closeness to London, has particular reason to honour him.

Richard Jefferies

Richard Jefferies, 1848–1887

One of the first people to appreciate the wonders of nature on the very doorstep of London, was that other "country writer," Richard Jefferies.

Born at Coate Farm in Swindon in 1848, Jefferies was to find the countryside around his birthplace a major source of inspiration. It informed the best-known of the nineteen books which he published during his lifetime, *Bevis: The Story of a Boy* (1882, a slightly fictionalised account of his childhood in nature) and *The Story of My Heart: An Autobiography* (1883, that rather overwrought *cri de coeur* against the modern mechanistic age). The farm now houses the Richard Jefferies Museum, and there is a bust of him in Salisbury Cathedral. Yet that bust is only a small version of the marble one in the National Portrait Gallery, and the fact is that most of his finest work was written away from his native Wiltshire, and a very significant part of it, in Surrey.

Jefferies' early life was quite different from Cobbett's. His father was an unsuccessful and impoverished farmer, while his mother, the daughter of a city book-binder, was fundamentally a Londoner—which perhaps explains why this writer never shared Cobbett's urge to grow things himself. A lonely and introspective child, he took solace in the glorious local downland, not rolling down a sandhill with his brothers like the boisterous young Cobbett, but stretching out alone on the grass to feel the earth enfolding him:

> I thought of the earth's firmness—I felt it bear me up; through the grassy couch there came an influence as if I could feel the great earth speaking to me. I thought of the wandering air—its pureness, which is its beauty; the air touched me, and gave me something of itself.... (*The Story of My Heart*, Chapter 1)

Despite the vague elemental longings which filled him, he also kept field notebooks, jotting down his close observations of the natural world around him. He liked reading, too, but there were few books at the farm, and he never attained anything like Cobbett's breadth of knowledge. As a teenager, he seemed to show something of Cobbett's adventurous spirit, and made a bold plan to go to Russia with a cousin. But this may only have been a symptom of the escapism which marks his more visionary work, and it had no practical results: the boys got no further than making the channel crossing to France, and failed again when they tried to set sail for the States from Liverpool.

Now, a writing career beckoned. Jefferies got his first job in 1866 as a reporter on the *North Wiltshire Herald*, moving on to the *Wiltshire and Gloucestershire Standard* in 1868. His first national publications were some clear-sighted letters to the *Times* on the hot topic of rural labourers, and three unsuccessful novels followed. It was time to move nearer the hub of literary England—especially as he now had a wife, Jessie, and a baby son, Harold, to support.

In the winter of 1876–7, when Jefferies was 28 or 29 (his birthday was in November), he took the big step of renting a house in Surbiton close to the Surrey/London boundary. Its address then was 2 Woodside, but it no longer backs on to trees, and is now known as 296 Ewell Road—the premises of Stack and Bonner estate agents, on a busy residential thoroughfare. A plaque was finally put up here for Jefferies in May 2003.

Although the neighbourhood is so built up now, we can still catch a glimpse of what it must have been like then. There is an area called Fishponds on the opposite side of the road, where old claypits have been filled with water to create a pleasant public park, and there are other patches of green around. Most important, the Hogsmill River, which rises in Ewell, is within two miles' walk. This was the location of two of the best essays in Jefferies' collection, *Nature near London*—"A Brook" and "A London Trout." Although he avoided naming places in his essays, believing, as he said in the preface to *Nature near London*, that "Everyone must find their own," the distinctive bridges across the river help to identify the ways he took. Happily, the Hogsmill is now the subject of a conservation project, and is already becoming a popular place for guided walks, since it has much of both natural and historic interest along the way.

A bridge over the Hogsmill: "There must be something in so sweet a stream"

The Surbiton years were momentous ones for the young couple. They had another child, a daughter called Jessie after her mother, but known by her second name, Phyllis. And here too Jefferies' literary career took off. No doubt it was handy to be closer to magazine editors and publishers. But the key factor in his success was that, in this setting, he was a countryman amongst Londoners, and this really defined him (both to himself and others) as a country writer. The timing was perfect, for, according to the contemporary English philosopher Roger Scruton, "the rural documentary had become the most popular form of non-fiction among the reading public—a position that it has retained to this day."[6] Articles drawing on Jefferies' Wiltshire experiences were snapped up by the *Pall Mall Gazette,* and then published in book form as *The Gamekeeper at Home* in 1878, to be followed by similar collections of essays, like *Wild Life in a Southern County* (1879) and *Round About a Great Estate* (1880). Also published in these years was the popular *Wood Magic: A Fable* (1881), which introduced his child-hero Bevis. And *Bevis* itself came out in three volumes in 1882, the year in which he left Surbiton and, after a summer in Exmoor, settled for a while in Brighton. Articles about the Surbiton area were reprinted in *Nature near London* (1883), the last chapters of which refer to Beachy Head, Ditchling Beacon and other Sussex landmarks.

Much of what Jefferies wrote in his productive Surbiton period harks back to his Wiltshire experience. Perhaps because he felt so cut off from it now, reading about it again in his notebooks brought it to his mind with crystal clarity. The cottagers, shepherds, poachers and other country folk he had known there, as well as the landscapes, flora and fauna he had loved so much, now sprang to life from his pen. Accuracy of description is only part of his skill. We are set down there ourselves, to tread right in his footsteps:

> Near the stream the ground is perhaps peaty; little black pools appear between tufts of grass, some of them streaked with a reddish or yellowish slime that glistens on the surface of the dark water; and as you step there is a hissing sound as the spongy earth yields, and a tiny spout is forced forth several yards distant.[7]

Yet while Jefferies recreated the past in such subtle and evocative detail, and in spite of his increasingly poor health, he made time for a daily walk around his new home, and found fresh subjects there too. Altogether twenty-five of his essays, most of them gathered in *Nature near London*, deal with this general locality, and their titles are listed in a pamphlet available from Kingston Museum. Here he is, characteristically intuitive and observant, looking over the edge of a particular bridge:

> There must be something in so sweet a stream. The sedges by the shore, the flags in the shallow, slowly waving from side to side with the current, the sedge-reedlings calling, the moorhens and water-rats, all gave an air of habitation.
> One morning ... something like a short thick dark stick drifted out from the arch, somewhat sideways.... The colour of the sides of the fish appeared at first not exactly uniform, and presently these indistinct differences resolved themselves into spots. It was a trout, perhaps a pound and a half in weight.

Again, we are involved in the very process of observation. The trout's fate soon hangs in the balance, as workmen dam the water beyond the bridge, and fishermen wade into the muddy shallows with an eel-spear at the ready.... Neither we nor Jefferies can bear to watch.

So involved do his readers become, that pinpointing the exact locations in these essays has developed into something of a sport for them. Edward Thomas, who wrote a full-length study of Jefferies, would have approved: "to explore the regions of Surrey where he roamed in his last healthy years ... is legitimate curiosity."[8] Thanks to his admirers' researches, it's now possible to trail him, for instance, along the road behind his house and across the Kingston by-pass into Woodstock Lane, and from there to Claygate, past Surbiton Golf Course and Telegraph Hill, and then back to his home. The place-names themselves reveal the contours of the past. Here, woods flourished once, and clay was removed to provide building material for new houses. Here, where the golf course was developed in 1895, Jefferies would have had open land to walk on. And here is the very hill from which telegraphic signals were sent, providing an early link between London and the south coast at Portsmouth. Even in its most suburban reaches, we can still find traces of the Surrey that Jefferies knew.

Like Cobbett, though, he did resent the way London was battening on the countryside. Telegraphs! He would make particular mention of them in *The Great Snow*, one of his two symbolic drownings of the city. In what seems to have been the first of these, only the dome of St Paul's is left visible above giant snowdrifts. This very short narrative ends abruptly with fanatics preaching to the troubled Londoners:

> "Where now," they cried, "Where now is your mighty city that defied nature and despised the conquered elements—where now is your pride when so simple and contemptible an agent as a few flakes of snow can utterly destroy it? Where are your steam-engines, your telegraphs and your printing-presses—all powerless, and against what—only a little snow!"

Far more important, however, is *After London*, which he published in 1885. With its odd mix of old-world feudalism and futurist prediction, this full-length novel is not to everyone's taste, yet it is a key text for science fiction and fantasy enthusiasts. Here, much of southern England is flooded after a catastrophe (a near-brush with some kind of meteor, perhaps), and becomes a beautiful, life-supporting lake—but London, at the lake's eastern end, is covered by slime and scum. Gases still bubble up from the decayed city beneath, and the hero of the second part of the story, Sir Felix Aquila, almost dies from these poisonous vapours while exploring the area. Jefferies blamed London for the decline in his own health, and he pours his bitterness into Chapter 23 of the novel, entitled "Strange Things," where Felix stumbles among nightmare scenes of skeleton imprints and blackened coins. Felix hopes to establish a very different way of life from that which lured people to the old city—a kind of rural utopia, in the idyllic region which he reaches soon afterwards. But we never know whether he achieves this or not. Jefferies leaves him setting off across a great trackless forest to fetch his beloved Lady Aurora. Maybe this hero's noble aspirations and romantic visions will triumph over the dangers ahead, and the degeneration of English society in general. He certainly walks off purposefully enough through the oak trees, much as Jefferies himself once walked through Surrey woodland to find respite from his own urban experience.

Not that Jefferies was implacably anti-London. Chapters 5 and 6 of *The Story of My Heart* tell of moments when he couldn't help responding to the vibrancy of the great metropolis. Yet, in the end, his visits there merely confirmed his need to be in touch with nature, and sharpened his profound conviction that such communion is vital to the soul.

In this respect, for all his idiosyncrasy as a writer, Jefferies was very much of his age. A contemporary of Thoreau and Whitman in America, he was also a forerunner of D.H. Lawrence and W.H. Hudson in England. "I am very fond of Jefferies," wrote Lawrence once, though he disliked *The Story of My Heart*, and was wary of such outpourings himself.[9]

After leaving Surbiton, Jefferies never lived anywhere else for any length of time. Having lost an infant son to meningitis, and growing ever weaker from the various symptoms of tuberculosis, he became more and more dispirited. Even the act of writing became such an effort that he had to dictate his later work to his wife. But, staring death in the face, he now understood clearly what his particular mission had been:

> Because my heart beats feebly to-day, my trickling pulse scarcely notating the passing of time, so much the more do I hope that those to come in future years may see wider and enjoy fuller than I have done; and so much the more gladly would I do all that I could to enlarge the life that shall be then.

It was in Surbiton that he had begun to fulfil this life-enhancing project.

In 1887, at the age of 38, Jefferies died at Goring-on-Sea on the south coast. There, where he had only been living a matter of months, "Jefferies House" now stands on "Jefferies' Lane." He was buried at the Broadwater Cemetery in Worthing, and became one of the first Victorian writers to have a society set up in his honour.

Considering the time he spent in Surbiton, and the amount he published in that time, Jefferies is still not as well remembered in Surrey as he might be. In fact, when the plaque over the Ewell Road estate agents was unveiled in 2003, local papers mistakenly described him as a poet. It was an interesting slip, which contains more than a grain of truth. At best, this writer's descriptions of the natural world *are* poetic—fresh, inspired, and raised from pure naturalism by a spiritual dimension. And no doubt it was his poetic tendencies that allowed him to give full rein to his apocalyptic vision, an aspect of his work that has always attracted its own special following.

Blue plaque to Jefferies at 196, Ewell Road

In the days of his health, a tall, stooped figure trekking across country with his flowing beard and his notebook in hand, Jefferies had been the very picture of an English nature-loving eccentric. Without such people both our literature and our whole culture would be much poorer. More specifically, by striding out into the Surrey area, he alerted his dedicated band of readers to the small, unnoticed wonders which still lie around us here every day. It's well worth reading Jefferies just to remember to look out for them. As he said, "You do not know what you may find each day; perhaps you may only pick up a fallen feather, but it is beautiful, every filament. Always beautiful!"

***

That Surrey should have had its share of country writers seems only right and proper. Just as predictable, perhaps, is the fact that *After London* was followed by further vindictive swampings of London by Surrey residents. The Canadian-born naturalist, popular scientist and novelist Grant Allen, who lived in Dorking for many years and died near Haslemere, published a story called "The Thames Valley Catastrophe" in *The Strand Magazine* of December 1897, in which a fiery flood of volcanic lava is spewed over the area. "There was no more London," he says emphatically. More recently, the first major novel of one of our foremost contemporary science-fiction writers, J.G. Ballard, was *The Drowned World* (1962), in which London is flooded by a more tropical and exotic swamp infested with iguanas and giant mosquitoes (a scenario less far-fetched than it sounds, since the Thames Barrier is already being challenged by rising sea levels, as a result of global warming). Ballard has lived in his unassuming semi-detached house near Shepperton station since 1960. Local writers with a visionary tendency seem irresistibly drawn to excising "the great Wen."

Notes to Chapter 3

[1] *A Tour through the Whole Island of Great Britain*, ed. P.N. Furbank, W.R. Owens and A.J. Coulson, New Haven & London, Yale University Press, 1991, pp.57–8.

[2] *Surrey: London's Southern Neighbour*, London: Hodder and Stoughton, 1938, p.124.

[3] *A Literary Pilgrim in England*, London: Cape, 1928, p.115.

[4] Unless otherwise specified, all quotations in this part of the chapter are from Cobbett's *Rural Rides*, edited by George Woodcock, Harmondsworth: Penguin, 1967.

[5] Written, coincidentally, in Farnham, where Swift had spent a number of years acting as a secretary to the diplomat Sir William Temple of Moor Park. However, it wasn't published until 1704, after he had left for Ireland. It was at Moor Park that Swift had met Esther Johnson, the "Stella" to whom he later wrote his *Journal to Stella* of 1710–1713.

[6] *England: An Elegy*, London: Chatto & Windus, 2000, p.235.

[7] Unless otherwise specified, all quotations in this part of the chapter are from *Landscape with Figures: An Anthology of Richard Jefferies's Prose*, edited by Richard Mabey, Harmondsworth: Penguin, 1983.

[8] *A Literary Pilgrim* (see note 3 above), p.137.

[9] See *The Letters of D.H. Lawrence, Vol. I, 1901–1913*, edited by James T. Boulton, Cambridge: Cambridge University Press, 1981, pp.137, 337 and 353, and *Vol. 2, 1913–1916*, edited by George J. Zytaruk and James T. Boulton, Cambridge: Cambridge University Press, p.243.

Suggested Reading

1. From Cobbett's *Rural Rides* (see note 4 above):
   November 29 (1822): the journey to Guildford, p.96 onwards
   October 27 (1825): Cobbett shows his eleven-year-old son Richard some of his old haunts in Farnham, p.248 onwards
   October 18 (1826): Cobbett, having passed through another bedroom on his way to breakfast, discusses his eating habits, p.447 onwards
2. George Spater's *William Cobbett: The Poor Man's Friend*, 2 Vols, Cambridge: Cambridge University Press, 1982, or Richard Ingrams' *Life and Adventures of William Cobbett*, London: HarperCollins, 2005.
3. *William Cobbett, 1763–1835*
   <www.blupete.com/Literature/Biographies/Reformers/Cobbett.htm>
4. From *Landscape with Figures* (see note 7 above):
   "Nightingales," about the catching of nightingales in Surrey for sale in London as songbirds, pp.184–7
   "A Brook—A London Trout," the full story of the trout (two essays combined), pp.136–52
   "Hours of Spring," a poignant essay written when Jefferies was confined to the house, pp.286–99
5. Jefferies' *After London or Wild England*, introduced by John Fowles, World's Classics, Oxford: Oxford University Press, 1980.
6. Edward Thomas' sympathetic but fair *Richard Jefferies*, London: Faber, 1978. This is still by far the best book on Jefferies.
7. Simon Coleman, *The Life and Works of Richard Jefferies*
   <www.bath.ac.uk/~lissmc/rjeffs.htm>

Places to Visit

For Cobbett:

Farnham Museum at Willmer House, 38 West Street, Farnham, has Cobbett's bust and memorabilia, and a pamphlet, "In the Steps of William Cobbett." Tel.0252 715094, Tues–Sat., 10am–5pm.

The William Cobbett, where Cobbett was born, is on Bridge Square, Farnham. Cobbett would have been born in the old white-washed and gabled part, to the right. There is a "Cobbett Corner" in the bar.

Cobbett's bust in the garden of the Museum of Farnham

71

Farnham Castle, where Cobbett worked in the gardens, offers guided tours. Tel. 0252 721194. According to Chris Howkins in *Hidden Surrey* (Newbury: Countryside, 1990), the best way to see Farnham is to come down to the castle from the north, on the A287, then continue downhill to the top of Castle Street.

St Andrew's Church has Cobbett's tomb outside, and a memorial plaque inside. This church is still kept open to the public.

*The National Portrait Gallery has a very fine painting of Cobbett, by George Cooke, in Room 20. It is said to show him in the clothes he wore for his trial in 1831.

For Jefferies:

296 Ewell Road, where Jefferies lived, is best reached by walking from the back of Surbiton Station, and taking a bus along Ewell Road in the direction of "Fishponds. " It is just an ordinary estate agent's office with a blue plaque above it.

Surbiton Public Library, about half a mile down the Ewell Road from Fishponds on the other side, has a commemorative plaque to Jefferies just inside the main entrance.

Carved wooden plaque to Richard Jefferies in Surbiton Library

A leaflet, **Richard Jefferies in Surbiton** (price 50p at time of writing) is available from Kingston Museum and Heritage Service, Wheatfield Way, Kingston-upon-Thames, Surrey KT1 2PS, Tel. 020-8547 6460.

A good way to celebrate Jefferies' connection with Surbiton is to take a walk, preferably one of the guided walking tours, along the Hogsmill. Free copies of a leaflet about this can be obtained from The Town Hall, The Parade, Epsom, Surrey, KT18 5BY (tel. 01372 732000). Enclose a self-addressed envelope and postage.

4. Excursions in the Countryside: Box Hill and the River Mole

Box Hill and Burford Bridge, c.1810

After passing through the countryside around Wotton, Cobbett crossed the River Mole on his second "rural ride" without comment, and with little more than a glance at Box Hill above him. Admittedly, the winter weather was ominous, and his mind was on the latest political scandal. Did he know that he was slighting England's very own Parnassus? Probably not. Yet here in mid-Surrey, not twenty miles from central London, is another place where the Muses have been worshipped, and returned the favour—not a mountain, exactly, but nevertheless a well-wooded hill at the end of the North Downs which has inspired some of our greatest literary figures.

Box Hill is only around 634 feet high, and not even the highest spot in the county. At 965 feet, Leith Hill, about three miles from Evelyn's Wotton, has that distinction. But Evelyn himself was quick to appreciate the lower rise's special qualities: "I went to Box Hill, to see those rare natural bowers, cabinets, and shady walks in the box-copses," he wrote in his diary for 27 August 1655. Even today, the hill is still clothed in beautiful, glossy-leaved evergreen box trees, planted by nature's hand amid majestic oaks, beech trees and whitebeams with their silver sheen in spring and summer, and red berries in winter. There are yews and junipers on its slopes as well, leading on one side down to that same Juniper Hall where Fanny Burney met her beloved French General. What's more, there is a glorious panoramic view from the top, still largely unspoiled. It spreads over the valley of the Mole (or the "Mole Gap") between Dorking and Leatherhead, where Great Bookham lies, and beyond—over Kent on one side, and Sussex on the other, taking in much of the so-called "Garden of England." Writers as well as artists have always been drawn to this lovely spot, which is now under National Trust management.

The stepping stones across the River Mole at the foot of Box Hill

Another mountain associated with the Muses in Greek mythology is Helicon, from which springs the sacred fountain of Hippocrene. Not to be outdone, Box Hill also has its special flow of fresh water, with spiritual associations and almost magical qualities.   The Mole, which Cobbett hastened across while lost in thought, was crossed here in prehistoric times by travellers on the trade route along the ridge of the North Downs. Then, in the Middle Ages, it is popularly supposed to have been crossed by pilgrims on the Surrey leg of the journey to St Thomas à Becket's tomb in Canterbury. Certainly there are stepping-stones between the banks which mark a ford here. The pretty river along what became known as the Pilgrims' Way has been written about by poets from at least Spenser onwards. Roughly fifty miles long, the Mole actually rises on the fringe of a runway at Gatwick Airport in Sussex, but by an accident of nature it really does appear to flow from Box Hill itself. This is because it has deep banks and sinks low into the porous chalk here, down deep holes which are famously known as "swallows," so that although the hill is actually the slope of its valley, antique maps show it emerging from the ground on either side.

Writers seem to have been fascinated by this. In Book 4 of *The Faerie Queene*, the sixteenth-century poet Edmund Spenser describes this strange burrowing (or "nousling") tendency:

Mole, that like a nousling Mole doth make

His way still under ground, till Thamis he ouer take.

(Canto xi poem 32)

Here, Spenser is drawing on the work of a poem entitled "Britannia," published by his contemporary William Camden in 1596. But, as a Londoner born and bred, and one who particularly loved the River Thames, he is generally assumed to have known the spot himself. Early in the next century, the topographical poet Michael Drayton is equally charmed by the habits of "the soft and gentle *Mole*," writing that the river

... digs her selfe a Path, by working day and night
(According to her name, to shew her nature right)
And underneath the Earth, for three miles space doth creep.

(Poly-Olbion, Song 17)

And a century later, Defoe, who had spent part of his boyhood at a small private school in nearby Dorking, explains more prosaically in his *Tour through the Whole Island of Great Britain*: "this river is called the Mole, from its remarkable sinking into the earth, at the foot of box-Hill...."[1]

Among the poets, John Milton was perhaps the only one to take a negative view of the phenomenon, describing "sullen Mole, that runneth underneath" in his 1628 part-Latin, part-English entertainment, "At a Vacation Exercise in the College." For the rest of the many authors who have enjoyed being in this part of the Surrey countryside, both hill and river have been wonderfully inspirational.

Jane Austen

As it happens, Box Hill's most famous appearance is in prose rather than poetry. Yet the outing to Box Hill in Jane Austen's *Emma* is more than just a key episode in that work. It hints at the romanticism which would colour the author's next and final novel, *Persuasion*.

Born in Steventon, near Basingstoke, Jane Austen (1775–1817) lived a much fuller life than we used to think. Far from staying at home in her father's Hampshire parsonage all the time, she travelled regularly and quite widely. As well as living in Southampton and Bath, she took many short trips with her family to relatives in London, Kent, Adlestrop in Gloucestershire, Stoneleigh Abbey in Warwickshire, Hamstall Ridware in Staffordshire, Lyme Regis (the setting of *Persuasion*)

Jane Austen, 1775–1817

and elsewhere on the Dorset coast, Devon, and maybe even Wales. When the family moved to Chawton in 1809, she was only about eight miles away from the Surrey border, by what is now the A31 to Farnham. It was from Chawton that she went to stay with her Surrey relatives the Cookes on her 1814 visit, and it was on her return to Chawton that she completed *Emma*, which was published late in the next year.

She was fond of Surrey. Although it was so close, the scenery there struck her as different and beautiful, as indeed it is. "I was very much pleased with the Country in general," she wrote of an earlier journey in May 1813, rhapsodising about the route through Surrey to London:

> between Guildford & Ripley I thought it particularly pretty, also about Painshill & every where else; & from a Mr Spicer's Grounds at Esher which we walked into before our dinner, the views were beautiful. I cannot say what we did *not* see, but I should think there could not be a Wood or a Meadow or a Palace or a remarkable spot in England that was not spread out before us, on one side or the other.[2]

Mr Spicer would have been John William Spicer, who bought the great estate of Esher Place in 1805, and who was known for opening his extensive grounds to visitors.[3] Although not mentioned here, Box Hill was only about eight miles away. Unmistakable in its outline, and close to their relatives in Great Bookham, it may have been one of the "remarkable spots" seen by the group from Hampshire.

Despite her earlier reluctance to visit the Cookes ("I assure You that I dread the idea of going to Bookham as much as you can do," she had written to her sister Cassandra beforehand), she seems to have found their place to her liking. *The Watsons*, an early fragment which has a heroine called Emma who attends a Surrey ball, shows that a Surrey novel was brewing in her mind long before she actually started *Emma*. Her memories of the county would have been refreshed by letters from the Cookes and meetings with them in Bath and London, and also by crossing the county again on her other travels. Within her more immediate family, too, she must have heard all about it. Her sister-in-law Eliza had a retreat in Dorking, which she called her "hermitage," just the name that Fanny Burney liked to use about her own various homes. And the Austens' Hampshire neighbour, Eliza Chute, had visited Box Hill and was brimming over with enthusiasm about it.[4] Once *Emma* was finally under way, Jane Austen was only too happy to accept another invitation to visit that part of the world.

There was no literary lion (or, rather, lioness) to put her off this time. Fanny Burney had moved on, and the only other writer in the neighbourhood now was the playwright Richard Brinsley Sheridan. He was the current owner of Polesden Lacey, the grand house just across from the d'Arblays' first home at Phoenice Farm. His plays had helped to inspire Austen's witty early work, *Lady Susan*, but she probably wouldn't have expected to meet such a personage. As for the Cookes themselves, they had won her gratitude by admiring "exceedingly" the recently published *Mansfield Park*. They approved of her treatment of the clergy in it, she explained to her sister. No doubt they also noted the novel's anti-slavery sentiments, so like those expressed in Mrs Cooke's own work, *Battleridge*. At any rate, Jane Austen looked forward to visiting the rectory of St Nicolas Church in Great Bookham in 1814, and even tried to persuade Cassandra to join her there.

Once there, according to a recent biographer, "she found her visit to the neighbourhood of Box Hill most useful for reviving memories of the local landscape."[5]

St Nicolas Church, Great Bookham,
where Jane Austen's godfather was once the vicar

Accuracy about the setting mattered to Jane Austen. We can see that from the way she picks holes in her niece Anna's manuscript: "Lyme will not do. Lyme is towards 40 miles distance from Dawlish & would not be talked of there," and so on. So it's no surprise to find that mid-Surrey is recreated perfectly in *Emma*. We know where we are long before she mentions a certain "Frank Churchill's stay in Surry" at the start of Chapter 30.

But we don't know *exactly* where we are. Emma Woodhouse's Highbury, described in the opening chapter as a "large and populous village almost amounting to a town" only sixteen miles from London, is thought by some to be modelled on Cobham. It's true that Cobham is the right distance from

London as well as Kingston, which various characters frequent on errands. It is also the right sort of size—that is to say, more "populous" than Great Bookham, which Fanny Burney had described as only a little village. Moreover, Mr Weston's kindness in reassuring the married Knightleys that there was "no scarlet fever in Cobham" (a slip of the pen for Highbury?) is remembered in Chapter 11. And Jane Austen certainly liked Cobham: a "very good Journey, & everything at Cobham was comfortable," she wrote on her own trip to London earlier that year. Supporters of Cobham's claims have found other clues, such as Randalls Road on the route from Cobham, its name tallying with that of the estate owned by the Westons in the novel. Yet Great Bookham itself is surely the stronger contender, and not only because Jane Austen actually stayed at the rectory there. Opposite the church, for example, is the Old Crown, rebuilt from an earlier pub of that name, and it is at an inn called the Crown that Emma and Mr Knightley take the floor together at Mr Weston's ball: "Brother and sister! No, indeed!" says Mr Knightley, as Emma accepts his hand (Chapter 38). This establishment is just where it should be, too—"a hop, step and jump" away from another old building with features closely resembling those of the Bates's home in the novel (Chapter 23). This is currently occupied by Lloyd's Bank, but it still has its old narrow staircase to the upstairs rooms, with a tricky "step at the turning" (Chapter 27).[6]

Suitable rooms for Miss Bates and her mother just "a hop, step and jump" away from the Crown in Great Bookham

Whichever mid-Surrey hamlet it brings to mind, Highbury is certainly pleasant. A little boring, perhaps, for a young person like Emma, but pleasant. Better, for sure, than anywhere else that her home-loving father can think of, and particularly lovely around the nearby estate of Mr George Knightley, with its "ample gardens stretching down to meadows washed by a stream," its "charming" lime-tree walk, and its "extremely pretty view" (Chapter 42). And it is, of course, an ideal place from which to visit the south-east's favourite vantage-point.

From the novelist's delight at Esher the year before, it appears that she had not yet seen the far more extensive panorama from Box Hill. This is hinted at in Chapter 42 itself: "Emma had not visited Box Hill yet; she wished to see what every body found so well worth seeing"—scarcely credible of a heroine living only a stone's throw away, but perfectly credible of a visitor from Hampshire, who had heard a neighbour enthusing about it and had had it pointed out to her from a distance.

As so often with much-anticipated outings, the morning spent on Box Hill in Chapter 43 is not a success. After the hustle and bustle of getting there, and the "burst of admiration" when the party finally arrives, the focus falls on human nature rather than the natural beauties of the scenery. And since the social mix is awkward, with tensions beneath the surface, human nature isn't seen at its best. On edge himself, Frank Churchill flatters Emma, and generally goads her into silly behaviour. As a result, Emma thoughtlessly mocks her dear old friend, Miss Bates, for her tiresomely rambling way of speaking. Mr Knightley's rebuke as she waits for her carriage shames and humiliates her, rousing emotions that are vital to the breakthrough in their relationship. Quite uncharacteristically, Emma weeps all the way home.

Nevertheless, the Surrey landscape does have its role in the chapter. For, towards the end of the two-hour stay on Box Hill, Emma herself tires of "flattery and merriment." Then, she wishes "herself rather walking quietly about with any of the others, or sitting almost alone, and quite unattended to, in tranquil observation of the beautiful views beneath her." In other words, she sees here that communing with nature, so particularly "beautiful" in such a spot, is better than that kind of false vivacity that Frank Churchill had inspired in her. This is hardly the first time that Jane Austen has given the nod to "sensibility." But here, in this most appealing of settings, she clearly recognises the part that nature can play in it. Where better for such a "romantic" realisation?

Emma was completed soon after the stay with the Cookes, although it was published only at the very end of the following year. Jane Austen was already at work on *Persuasion* by then, a novel of nearly-lost love which seems to come more directly from her heart than any other. It is a work which does much to refute Charlotte Brontë's criticism that her writings lack passion and poetry. The author of *Jane Eyre* complains that that there is "no open country—no fresh air—no blue hill—no bonny beck" in *Pride and Prejudice*.[7] But the earlier novelist's characters do venture out of their confined homes in *Emma*, and they find all these things in lovely mid-Surrey. Her next heroine Anne Elliot goes further afield, admiring the sea, the cliffs and even the "green chasms between romantic rocks" on the Dorset coast, and the forest trees and lush orchards inland. Anne feels that here one could sit by the sea in "unwearied contemplation" (Chapter 11), yet in the following chapter, the breeze whips colour and animation into her face. In *Persuasion*, therefore, there's a real sense of interaction between human nature and external nature, and of responsiveness to nature as a determinant of character. The Box Hill episode can be seen as an important step towards this most romantic of Jane Austen's novels—her swan song, where nature features not in all its fresh summer glory, to be sure, but with the poignant late bloom of autumn.

John Keats

John Keats, 1795–1821

On the afternoon of Saturday 22 November 1817, little more than three years after Jane Austen's stay in Great Bookham, and just three months after her death, a young Londoner set out for Box Hill on the London-Portsmouth coach. He was a poet—though by no means the first of the romantic poets to seek out the area. Among the earlier ones were William Wordsworth, whose friend Francis Wragham was a curate at Cobham, and who had gone there from London in 1795, and Anna Laetitia Barbauld, who had written to a friend in September 1805 that she and her husband had been staying at "a little quiet sort of an inn in the centre of the pleasant walks; and a few days with our friends the C- - - -s."[8] (Surely, the literary Cookes again?) However, for this poet the visit to Box Hill was going to be especially important.

John Keats (1795–1821) was only twenty-two years old, but he was at a difficult point in his life. He had already known much sadness. When he was eight, his father, a livery stable manager in Moorfields in the heart of the city of London, had died after falling off a horse. Six years later, his mother had died of tuberculosis. He had been left poor, and with a dread of facing an early death himself. Only the year before, he'd given up a promising career in medicine to devote himself to poetry. Now he was struggling with his first full-scale poetic work, a reworking of the Greek legend about Endymion, the shepherd-prince beloved of the goddess of the moon. The poem starts with the well-known lines,

> A thing of beauty is a joy forever:
> Its loveliness increases; it will never

Pass into nothingness; but still will keep
A bower quiet for us, and a sleep
Full of sweet dreams, and health, and quiet breathing....

But now Keats was worried about "the winding up"[9] of what had become an elaborate allegory of the quest for the ideal.

The Burford Bridge Hotel today.
Keats stayed here in 1817 when it was The Fox and Hounds

After alighting at Burford Bridge, close to the stepping stones across the Mole, he checked into the Fox & Hounds—the same hostelry at which the Barbaulds had stayed. He had probably heard about it from his friend William Hazlitt, who had also been a guest there. Taking a room at the back overlooking the stables, he set off with characteristic impetuousness to climb the hill that very evening. "I like this place very much," he enthused in a letter to his friend J.H. Reynolds on his return. "There is Hill and Dale and a little River—I went up Box hill this Evening after the Moon—you a'seen the Moon—came down—wrote some lines."

"You a'seen the Moon" means "You should have seen the Moon," and is an exclamation of delight. Clearly, the moonlit scenery chimed well with the mood of his unfinished poem. The concluding part of "Endymion," Book IV, opens with an invocation which sounds triumphant rather than pleading:

Muse of my native land! Loftiest Muse!
O first-born on the mountains!

Having found the inspiration he had longed for, he worked frantically on the poem over the next few days. One particular passage in this last part, with its references to a "steep mossy hill" with "dark yew trees" which "drop their scarlet berry cups of dew," and a "crystal rill," could hardly have been written anywhere else. "O thou wouldst joy to live in such a place," Endymion tells his beloved. Keats would complete the poem on 28 November.

But first, before he went to bed that first night, Keats wrote another letter besides the one to Reynolds. This one was to his close friend, Benjamin Bailey, then an Oxford undergraduate. And in his exalted mood he expressed himself particularly memorably:

> I am certain of nothing but of the holiness of the Heart's affections and the truth of Imagination—What the imagination seizes as Beauty must be truth.... The Imagination may be compared to Adam's dream—he awoke and found it truth.

These words were once sold as a decorated text at the Keats House in Hampstead, where he moved a year later, in December 1818. Equally well known, however, is Keats's heartfelt cry later in the letter, "O for a Life of Sensations rather than of Thoughts!" Then there's his plaintive comment towards the end, "I scarcely remember counting upon any Happiness...." But, he goes on, with the view from Box Hill evidently still fresh in his mind, "the setting sun will always set me to rights." And he gives another example of how he can lose himself in external nature: "or if a sparrow come before my Window I take part in its existence and pick about the gravel." Here he is expressing his capacity for empathy, or what he would call later, "negative capability." This is a wonderful letter, even more important perhaps than the poem he now felt able to finish. Keats's first evening at Box Hill was clearly one of the high points of this young poet's new and unfolding career as a man of letters.

Indeed, Keats liked the spot so much that he decided to stay on even after completing "Endymion"—right into December. He spent the time wandering by the Mole and on Box Hill itself. At the turn of the month, he saw the change in the scenery, and composed another poem, a short one this time, about it. Although the title "Stanzas" ("In a drear-nighted December") sounds uninspired and dull, it is a moving poem, which is often anthologised. Here is the first of the three stanzas, in which the poet notes that despite its bare wintry branches, a representative deciduous tree seems "happy":

> In a drear-nighted December,
>   Too happy, happy tree,
> Thy branches ne'er remember
>   Their green felicity.
> The north cannot undo them,
> With a sleety whistle through them;
> Nor frozen thawings glue them
>   From budding at the prime.

Some of the words here, like "Too happy, happy tree," look forward to his later, more celebrated poetry—"Ode on a Grecian Urn," for instance, with its "happy, happy boughs." More important, though, is the implied comparison of nature and human beings. Nature lives only in the present moment, but is guaranteed seasonal renewal. Human beings, on the other hand, with their keen sensitivity to change, are not. The second stanza is about the river, which also benefits from the "sweet forgetting" of nature. But it's the third and final stanza which makes the contrast with humanity explicit. Here, Keats points out how painful it is for us (especially, it seems, separated lovers) to recall past happiness, and concludes that

> The feel of not to feel it,
> When there is none to heal it,
> Nor numbèd sense to steel it,
> Was never said in rhyme.

The torment of loss was always an important theme for Keats, whose brother Tom's health was already giving way. Tom Keats would die exactly a year later from the same disease that carried off their mother. This theme would find even more haunting expression in the great poems still to come, like "Ode to a Nightingale."

Box Hill and the Mole having worked their magic on him, Keats returned to London early in December 1817 to fulfil his early promise, and to become, in the few years remaining to him, one of the best-loved of all English poets.

*****

Over the years, Box Hill has attracted many other literary figures.

A forgotten star of the pre-Victorian period, Richard "Conversation" Sharp was a rich hat-maker turned critic and politician, whose wit and hospitality attracted a host of literary celebrities to Fredley Manor, his Box Hill home opposite Juniper Hall. These visitors included Sir Walter Scott, the Poet Laureate Robert Southey, and Southey's sister-in-law's husband, Samuel Taylor Coleridge. John Stuart Mill also lived nearby in the nineteenth century, and tried hard but unsuccessfully to prevent the railway running through a part of Norbury Park. He became the founder of the Commons Preservation Society, presumably after becoming less staunchly Utilitarianist.

Later still came the novelist and poet George Meredith, the subject of my next chapter, who took up residence in grey Flint Cottage on the lower slopes of the hill for the last thirty years of his life. He would trek from there right across the county and beyond, with the most illustrious rambling group ever known: the "Sunday Tramps," founded by Sir Leslie Stephen, co-editor of the *Dictionary of National Biography*, and the father of Virginia Woolf.

Nearby, at Fern Dell on the London-Dorking Road, lived the Scottish poet

Charles Mackay, whose daughter was to adopt the name Marie Corelli, and become an immensely successful popular novelist. At the time, Meredith encouraged the girl in her musical ambitions, but his actual example as a writer seems to have been much more potent, and no wonder. He was the epitome of a Grand Old Man of Letters by then, and his home turned into a place of "pious pilgrimage" for the literati of the time. Those words were Flora Thompson's, about her own expedition to Flint Cottage around 1899 long before she herself was known as an author. She wasn't able to "catch a glimpse of her idol,"[10] but others were more favoured—people such as Thomas Hardy, Henry James, Rudyard Kipling, J.M. Barrie, Robert Louis Stevenson, and H.G. Wells, all beat a path to his door—Wells having been summoned, not long before Meredith's death, to hear an idea for a science fiction story.

Stevenson, better known for his travels to more exotic places, seems to have liked Surrey, for he stayed for several months in 1878/9 at the Fox & Hounds at Burford Bridge. He is said to have written one of the best-known poems in his *Child's Garden of Verses* at Box Hill, after hearing the old wives' tale that the shutters rattled at night because a mysterious rider was passing by:

> Whenever the moon and the stars are set,
>   Whenever the wind is high,
> All night long in the dark and wet,
>   A man goes riding by.
> Late in the night when the fires are out,
> Why does he gallop and gallop about?
>   "Windy Nights"

It's fun to know that this popular little verse probably has a local connection. In the early 1880s Stevenson spent some time at the Hand & Spear in nearby Weybridge as well, which accounts for an unexpected item once exhibited in the Elmbridge Museum there—the writing desk at which he corrected the first batch of proofs for *Treasure Island*.

Correcting proofs is drudgery, as Stevenson himself apparently felt. A far more glamorous event took place at Box Hill itself, in what was now called the Hare & Hounds, in June 1895. This was a dinner of the prestigious Omar Khayyám Society, the first (honorary) president of which had been the *Rubáiyát*'s translator Edward FitzGerald. Thomas Hardy was a founder-member. On this particular occasion, the society was meeting to honour Meredith, who was now an invalid, and Meredith and Hardy each made a speech. Hardy's second wife Florence comments that it was "said to be the first and last ever made by either of them; at any rate, it was the first, and last but one or two, by Hardy."[11] Surely this was the high point in the history of England's very own Parnassus—these two literary giants taking the floor in front of the intellectual élite of their day, as the breeze rustled in the fine old trees outside, and the "nousling Mole" went murmuring by.

Hardy's work has stood the test of time much better than Meredith's. But to imagine each of them speaking is to realise something at once. Without Meredith's idiosyncratic, demanding but often captivating style, as well as Hardy's more sombre iconoclasm, the novel might never have become the thriving and versatile form that it is today.

The same might be said, of course, for D.H. Lawrence, who opened up the novel's possibilities in his own way. And, yes, he too came to Box Hill. He was living in Croydon at the time of Meredith's death, putting some of his vivid life into his teaching job at an elementary school there. Though he taught his young pupils with characteristic vigour, and laughed with them and loved them, he was drained by the end of the day ("despoiled … a mere blossomless husk," as he put it himself in a poem entitled "After School") and needed to get away sometimes and roam in more rural parts of Surrey. "Down here it is wonderful," he wrote on a postcard of Mickleham Church on November 1908:

The masses of gorgeous foliage, the sharp hills whose scarps are blazing with Autumn, the round valleys where the vivid dregs of Summer have collected—they have almost intoxicated me.

So much of Lawrence is there, both as a nature-lover and a writer, in that scrawled note. On another postcard from the area, he commented more prosaically to a friend, "I should love you to ride with me through Surrey—it is a most sweet and lovely county."[12]

Finally, another writer with a different kind of reputation hiked his way to Box Hill in the early twentieth century. This was Hilaire Belloc, best remembered now for his *Cautionary Tales* of 1908. In fact, Belloc did much more than simply compose limericks. He had been a brilliant undergraduate at Oxford, and went on to write not only serious poetry, but also novels, biographies, histories, essays of all kinds—and travel books. He was in his late thirties when he hit upon the idea of walking the length of the legendary Pilgrims' Way. "For my part I desired to step exactly in the footprints of such ancestors," he explained.[13]

The book that grew out of his trek was *The Old Road*, published in 1910. Box Hill was, of course, an important landmark on his route, a fact which Belloc fully appreciated. The hill "attracted and held the sight as one looked eastward," he said, declaring it "the strongest and most simple of our southern hills," and describing how "it occupies the landscape alone." Aptly enough, he called the steep rise which ends so abruptly with the Mole valley "the Cape of Box Hill." Its dramatic, or even romantic, quality as a river cliff (which is how geologists refer to it) evidently appealed to him. And although he himself was concerned with more distant times, many years before even Spenser arrived on the scene, what he said about his own researches applies to anyone interested in recovering the past associations of such a wonderful place, literary or otherwise: "Reverence and knowledge and security and the love of a good land—all these are increased or given by the pursuit of this kind of learning."

The "Old Road" as it passes through Compton

Notes to Chapter 4

[1] *A Tour through the Whole Island of Great Britain*, edited by P.R. Furbank and W.R. Owens and A.J. Coulson, New Haven and London: Yale University Press, 1991, p.60.

[2] *Jane Austen's Letters*, edited by Deirdre le Faye, 3rd edition, Oxford: Oxford University Press, 1997, p.210. Later page references in this section of the chapter are all to this edition.

[3] Interestingly, the Spicers were also friendly with Jane and Anna Maria Porter, sisters who lived in Esher and wrote mainly historical romances (well-known then, but, like Mrs Cooke's, all but forgotten now). Mr Spicer would no doubt have been delighted to know that on this occasion he was entertaining someone whose fame would one day be much greater. I am indebted to Chris Cowell for information about the Spicers and the Porters.

[4] See Claire Tomalin's *Jane Austen: A Life*, Harmondsworth: Penguin, 1998, p.96.
[5] David Nokes, *Jane Austen*, London: Fourth Estate, 1997, p.443.
[6] I am indebted to local historian Libby Matts for this information.
[7] *The Letters of Charlotte Brontë, with a Selection of Letters by Family and Friends*, edited by Margaret Smith, Vol.2, 1848–1851, Oxford: Clarendon, 2000, p.10.
[8] *A Memoir of Mrs Anna Laetitia Barbauld, with Many of Her Letters*, edited by Grace A. Ellis, 2 vols, Vol.1, Boston: Osgood, 1874, p.257.
[9] Letter to J.H. Reynolds, *John Keats, 1814–1821: Selected Letters*, Oxford: Oxford University Press, 2002, pp.35–8. All quotations in this section of the chapter are from this edition unless otherwise specified.
[10] *Heatherley*, published with notes by John Owen Smith, Headley Down, 1998, pp.32–33.
[11] *The Life of Thomas Hardy*, London: Studio Editions, 1994, p.37.
[12] *The Letters of D.H. Lawrence, Vol. I, 1901–1913*, edited by James T. Boulton, Cambridge: Cambridge University Press, 1979, pp.90–91.
[13] *The Old Road*, London: Constable, 1910, p.9. All quotations in this section of the chapter are from this edition unless otherwise specified. For a sceptical look at the Pilgrims' Way, see Matthew Alexander's *Tales of Old Surrey* (Newbury: Countryside, 1985), pp.20–22.

Suggested Reading

1. Jane Austen's *Emma* (see especially Chapters 42 and 43).
2. Claire Tomalin's *Jane Austen: A Life*, Harmondsworth: Penguin, 1998.
3. Keats's *Endymion*, Book 4, particularly lines 670–721, in which Endymion tries to entice his beloved with offers of an earthly paradise. (A collected edition of the poems, such as H.W. Garrod's 1970 Oxford Paperback edition, is needed for this.)
4. Keats's letter of November 22, 1817, *Selected Letters* (see note 9 above).
5. Keats's "Stanzas" ("In a drear-nighted December").
6. Stephen Coote's *John Keats: A Life*, London: Hodder (Sceptre paperback), 1996, especially pp.103–6, or Andrew Motion's *Keats*, London: Faber, 1997, especially pp.207–12.

Places to Visit

Box Hill, or Boxhill as it is also written, can be reached by the car or train, because Westhumble & Boxhill station is just over the road from the hotel, by an underpass. There is a National Trust shop and Information Centre at the top.

The Fox & Hounds, which became the Hare & Hounds in 1882, is just at the foot of the hill. It is now known simply as the Burford Bridge Hotel, and its postal address is actually: The Foot of Boxhill, Dorking, Surrey RH5 6BX. Tel. 0870 400 8283. Complete with Keats and Lady Hamilton rooms (Nelson and Emma

Hamilton spent some of their last hours here before Nelson left for the Battle of Trafalgar), as well as a minstrel's gallery, it is a Heritage hotel, belonging to the Forte group.

There are two planned walking routes around the Box Hill area itself:
i) A literary walk which starts at the Box Hill car park off the A24, nearly opposite the Burford Bridge Hotel. (Sharp's Fredley Manor, Meredith's Flint Cottage and the site of Mackay's Fern Dell can all be seen on this route, as can the spot at Burford Corner where Defoe is once thought to have lived.)
ii) A community walk which starts at Westhumble & Boxhill station, and goes past the plaque to Fanny Burney and on to Polesden Lacey. Here, the original long terrace which Sheridan extended can still be found. It has yew trees along it and two pieces of stone statuary with passages of poetry on their plinths (see frontispiece). However, the house itself has been completely rebuilt since Sheridan's time (it is a Regency villa where the late Queen Mother spent part of her honeymoon). The gardens are open all the year round. Part of the North Downs Way is signposted along this walk.
See <www.bbc.co.uk/southerncounties/community/walks/boxhill.shtml>
**Note that the famous "Zig Zag" road up Box Hill is very popular with bikers, mainly on Sundays and public holidays. This detracts from the atmosphere a bit!

Dorking and District Museum, tucked away at The Old Foundry, 62 West Street in Dorking Town centre, has a marvellous archive of books, newspaper-clippings, etc. Open Wed. and Thurs. 2–5pm and Sat. 10am–4pm. Tel. 01306 876591.

Great Bookham, where Jane Austen stayed with the Cookes, is just a few miles away. It was listed at the end of Chapter 2 in connection with Fanny Burney, but is of interest to Jane Austen fans too. As well as the wall plaque to her godfather, the Reverend Samuel Cooke, the parish church of St Nicolas has a brass depicting the arms of a family called the Westons (on the north wall of the Slyfield Chapel, as explained near the Book of Remembrance at the other end of the church). The inn which is now called The Old Crown is at 1, High Street, with the Lloyd's Bank building, which is said to be perfect for the Bates's home, just over the road.

Cobham, with its old part at the end of the High Street (the area around the church and along the Tilt, including old inns and a working water mill on the Mole), is also worth seeing in connection with Jane Austen, as the old part along the Mole is much as she would have known it (minus the traffic, of course). Painshill, which she mentions in her May 1813 letter, is a magnificent eighteenth-century landscape garden on its outskirts, at the junction of the A3 and A245. Nearest train station: Cobham. It has a Gothic temple, tower, grotto, and so on, and a beautiful lake (more about that at the end of the next chapter). The River Mole winds around the grounds. Entry times change with the season and need to be checked.
<www.aboutbritain.com/Painshillpark.htm> Tel.01932 868113.

Keats House in London is beside Hampstead Heath, near Hampstead Heath or Belsize Park tube stations, open to all visitors from noon to 5pm, except Mondays. Tel. 020 7435 2062.

*Jane Austen's *Chawton* is very close to Surrey, too, but on its south-western border. It can be reached by road from Farnham or Alton, or by train from Waterloo to Alton, only about a mile away. Tel. 01420 83262.

5. Another Side to Matthew Arnold

Matthew Arnold, 1822–1888

In his portrait by the famous Victorian artist and sculptor George Frederic Watts, Matthew Arnold (1822–1888) sports a centre parting, side-whiskers and stiff collar, and looks every inch the austere and unbending Victorian gentleman. Yet, like so many other spokesmen of his generation, the author of such major works as "The Scholar Gipsy" and *Culture and Anarchy* had another side to him—a side which can now be seen only in his letters.

For a long time, it was hardly possible to see it even there. Both his widow and his surviving sister made cuts to the letters before they were first published, and between them they removed the affectionate words of a loving husband, and "every trace of humour." The result, as the editor of this original two-volume collection himself realised, "was a curious obscuration of some of Arnold's most characteristic traits—such, for example, as his overflowing gaiety."[1]

Recently, however, an "unexpurgated" six-volume edition of his

90

correspondence has shown the famous poet and critic as he really was. Gone is the nostalgic, backward-looking atmosphere of so much of his poetry. Gone too is the "high seriousness" (one of his own favourite terms) of his critical essays. Instead, he writes to his nearest and dearest with unshadowed delight about the minutiae of his daily life, particularly, as time goes by, about his life in the Surrey countryside. In these letters, and against this lovely backdrop, "the kindness, the homeliness, the unaffected simplicity of Mr Arnold's bright and happy nature"[2] are fully revealed at last.

Matthew Arnold is most commonly associated with three different parts of England—Rugby, the Lake District, and Oxford. As a boy, he was a pupil at Rugby, where his father was the great headmaster, and as a young man he briefly taught classics there himself. All through his life, he took holidays at Fox How, the family's grey ten-bedroomed mansion in Ambleside, built in 1834 with the advice of William Wordsworth. Fox How was owned by the family for almost a hundred years, and still stands as a monument to the fading gleams of the Romantic era in that beautiful landscape. Arnold also followed in his father's footsteps by making a name for himself at Oxford, winning the prestigious Newdigate Prize as an undergraduate, becoming a fellow at Oriel, and later being elected Professor of Poetry at Oxford for two five-year terms. Not only "The Scholar Gipsy" but also several of his other poems are set in the Oxfordshire countryside.

Yet his strongest ties were always with the south-east. He was born in the little Thames-side village of Laleham on Christmas Eve 1822, and christened in the parish church of All Saints, Laleham, on 23 January 1823. Laleham was in Middlesex then, but fought successfully to be annexed to Surrey rather than Greater London when Middlesex was abolished as a county in 1965. It was in present-day Surrey, therefore, that Matthew spent much of his childhood. And he chose to live for the last fifteen years of his life in Cobham, only about six miles away from Laleham, but so quintessentially and traditionally "Surrey" that, as we have seen, it is considered to be a possible model for Jane Austen's Highbury in *Emma*. The poet Edward Thomas, himself highly attuned to the connection of man and nature, felt that only here in Cobham could the younger Arnold "really be seen at home."[3]

The family's links with this corner of England began before his birth, when Arnold's father, the brilliant and idealistic Thomas Arnold, came to Laleham in 1819 to start his teaching career. He was then unmarried, but arrived with his married sister Frances and her husband, the Reverend John Buckland, and brought over to Laleham a whole troupe of Arnolds—his widowed mother, his aunt Susan, and another sister, Susannah, who was an invalid. No plaque commemorates the site of the large brick house which he rented on Laleham Broadway, and where his first son, Matthew, would be born. After the house itself was demolished in 1864, it was replaced by a vicarage, which is now used as a nursing home for the elderly, called the Glebe House Residential Home. However, local children go on from the adjacent primary school to the Matthew Arnold School a short distance away in Staines, so the connection with the author in the family is not forgotten.

At this time, fresh from studying theology at Oxford, Thomas Arnold had agreed to help his brother-in-law set up a preparatory school. Finding the right premises had proved difficult, and the two brothers-in-law had fixed on the area "almost as a last desperate chance." Yet Thomas Arnold was quite satisfied with his new surroundings, painting a picture of it as it was when his children grew up there:

> This Place is really a quiet Village and not at all infested with Cockneys and with no coach passing through it; it is very small and being situated on the Thames it is very convenient for pleasant walks as well as for bathing and punting....

He particularly enjoyed exploring "on the Surrey side," writing:

> It is very beautiful, and some of the scenes at the junction of the heath country with the rich valley of the Thames are very striking. ... the bank of the river up to Staines ... though it be perfectly flat, has yet a great charm from its entire loneliness, there being not a house anywhere near it.

Arnold would gather the older scholars around him at his redbrick house, while the building acquired for the younger boys was Muncaster House on Ferry Lane, on the opposite side of Laleham, and leading down to the river. It certainly looks the part, although it has now been turned into flats.

Muncaster House, Laleham

A great deal of work had to be done to prepare it for its first pupils, and Buckland seems to have been the one to do it. Thomas Arnold wrote from there, to a friend in Oxford, "He made a very good School Room out of the Root House."[4] The Root House would have meant the vegetable store, and young Matthew Arnold would one day be taught there himself.

It was common enough for clerics to tutor boys privately, but Buckland's school could take about thirty pupils, and was the country's first true "Prep School." Next to the Matthew Arnold School in Staines are the Buckland Junior and Infant Schools, so this has not been forgotten, either. However, reputations are not built overnight. Thomas Arnold only had a handful of older boys, and had to borrow money when he got married a year later to a clergyman's daughter, Mary. The first of their six children to start their lives at the house on Laleham Broadway was a girl, Jane. Matthew, the future poet and critic, was the next.

Matthew is said to have been rather a troublesome child, and he had some problem with his legs as well, making it necessary for him to wear heavy leg-irons. It's touching to imagine him dragging himself about Laleham in these. "I cannot help thinking that they would have been equally safe and efficacious if *much* lighter," his anxious mother wrote in her journal in June 1826.[5] His clumsy way of walking continued even after the leg-irons came off, and earned him the nickname "Crabby."

Matthew Arnold's early childhood in Laleham was tough in another way. His father demanded as much from his children as his pupils. He employed a series of governesses for them, but he was the one who directed their studies. They had to learn Latin grammar, French verbs and so on when they were five, and Greek, German and Italian from the age of six. (No wonder Matthew Arnold's criticism and published notebooks are peppered with quotations in various languages!) Then their father would test them on Sunday evenings, something which their mother later remembered fondly, but which may have been much less fun for the children.

For Matthew, at least, Laleham remained a base even after his father's appointment as the headmaster of Rugby School. With great reluctance, his immediate family did move there after nine years, but the rest of the Arnold clan remained in Laleham with the Bucklands, and Matthew himself was soon sent back to be taught at his uncle's school. He hated being apart from his parents, and felt confined by the school's strict routine. Progress was slow, and his father had to write to him in Laleham to scold and encourage him. After two years, he was able to rejoin his parents. Still, his links with Laleham were maintained. For example, when he burnt his hand once, it was to his aunt at Laleham that his parents sent him to recover.

Much as he had disliked the Muncaster House school, Matthew Arnold loved the neighbourhood itself. It continued to beckon him when he was grown up. He was there visiting his aunt at New Year in 1848, when he was 25 and working in London as Private Secretary to Lord Lansdowne—his first job. On Sunday 2 January he attended a service at the little old brick church where he had been christened, reporting to his mother in Rugby that he went along the "shelving gravelly road up towards Laleham," to find the stream at

Penton Hook, where the Thames makes a hook-like loop just north-west of Laleham, "with the old volume, width, shine, rapid fullness … unchanged & unequalled." He also mentions nostalgically "the heaths and pines of Surrey." In August 1849 he was there walking up the riverbank again with his uncle and other family members, at the head of his uncle's pupils. "It changes less than any place I ever go to," he wrote to his sister. The next morning, he went diving and swimming in the river "with the swans looking at me" together with his old schoolfriend from Rugby, Thomas Hughes, the author of *Tom Brown's Schooldays*. Hughes was exactly his age, and a great fan of his father's. He must have been delighted to visit the scenes of his beloved headmaster's early manhood.

"It changes less than any place I ever go to": the Thames at Laleham

This was the very year in which Arnold's first book of poems, *The Strayed Reveller and Other Poems*, was published. It contained his ever-popular "The Forsaken Merman" with its seaside setting, but in which, too, the voices of the children and the "sweet airs" wafted "seaward / From heaths starr'd with broom" recall his Laleham past. A stanza in "Lines Written in Kensington Gardens" in his next volume (*Empedocles on Etna and other poems*, 1852), suggests just how deeply this past affected him:

> In the huge world which roars hard by
> Be others happy, if they can!
> But in my helpless cradle I
> Was breathed on by the rural Pan.

Coming from such a background, the speaker in this short poem delights in the "red-boled" pines, daisies and thrushes around him in the popular London park. He goes on to pray to the "Calm soul of all things" for the ability to respond wholeheartedly to the peace which it gives here (a peace which

"Man did not make and cannot mar!") and for a quiet mind, a sympathetic heart, and a full life. This is the poem of a young man at the start of his adulthood, in which Wordsworthian ideas spring to life with fresh details and a very personal prayer. The last part of the prayer ("nor let me die / Before I have begun to live") is especially poignant: Arnold's father had died suddenly ten years before, at the age of forty-six.

In stanza five of "Lines Written in Kensington Gardens" Arnold compares the "fragrant grass" at his feet with that upon which an angler might recline by a stream, to count his catch. The riverside environment of his boyhood had become the landscape of his mind, and often appears in his imagery. "The Buried Life," for instance, is an archetypal Victorian poem in which he is aware of the undertow of the soul's true current, and appreciates those rare moments when a loved one distracts us from "the rush and glare" of our busy lives, and puts us back in touch with it. Then, "a lost pulse of feeling stirs again," so that

> A man becomes aware of his life's flow,
> And hears its winding murmur; and he sees
> The meadow where it glides, the sun, the breeze.

"The Future" develops the life/river metaphor more schematically, as man's voyage continues from the river's source to the ocean. The crowding in of cities on its banks is noted with foreboding and anxiety, but as the flow widens again, the "Murmurs and scents of the infinite Sea" bring hopes of peace. Arnold's poetic masterpiece of 1853, "The Scholar Gipsy," based on a seventeenth-century tale about an Oxford scholar who opted out of society, is set around the Oxfordshire stretch of the Thames. Yet here too the best-known stanza (stanza 21) uses the river figuratively, to suggest the joys of the past, when "life ran gaily as the sparkling Thames" before the advent of "this strange disease of modern life." This river could be the Thames anywhere—at Laleham, even, for nowhere does Arnold associate himself more wistfully with his "truant boy" hero than here.

By this time, Arnold was already burdened by responsibilities. He had married Frances Lucy (Flu) in 1851, and their first son Thomas had already been born. Their second, Trevenen ("Budge"), was on the way. And just before his marriage he had become an Inspector of Schools, a job which involved checking elementary school and teacher standards all over the country, and even travelling on the continent, to see how things were being done over there. His references in "The Scholar Gipsy" to "sick hurry ... divided aims ... heads o'ertaxed" do seem to reflect his struggles at this point in his life.

Arnold would always be busy, always energetically involved in the world. It was years before the couple even had a proper base, finally settling down for about eight years near Flu's parents in London's Belgravia. By now they had another son, Richard, and the family was still growing. Poetry began to seem a self-indulgence, for which Arnold's school-visiting, school reports and pupil-teacher examining, as well as his Oxford lectures, left him little leisure. Perhaps, too, using his critical faculties all the time kept inspiration at bay, or undermined his confidence as a poet. Whatever the reason or reasons, he published his last book of poems only a year after completing his second stint as Professor of Poetry at Oxford in 1868. In 1871, he became a Senior Inspector of Schools, and in 1884 his title was changed to that of Chief Inspector. He retired from his demanding work slightly less than a year before his death.

All Saints, the little brick church at Laleham

During middle age, Arnold had particular cause to revisit Laleham on several occasions. The male Arnolds were not robust. He and Flu lost three of their four sons. Their youngest boy, Basil, died at the age of sixteen months in January 1868. That March, the family moved to Harrow, which was convenient for Arnold's current school district, as well as being close to Harrow School for the remaining boys. But later in the same year, just as he was preparing the influential essays of *Culture and Anarchy* for publication, Thomas died too, to be followed all too soon by Budge. At first, Ambleside had been considered for Basil's resting place, but in the end the three boys were buried under one vault at Laleham, for which, Arnold confessed, " I ... shall always have a home feeling."

On a far happier note, while they were living in Belgravia, the family had twice taken advantage of the new railway station at Dorking to spend holidays in Westhumble, where Arnold had been "perfectly astonished" by the beauty of the Box Hill area, and had mentioned that Thackeray's daughters were staying close by as well. The "yews, boxes, limes and beeches of Norbury" had enchanted him. When he made up his mind to leave Harrow with its painful memories, he naturally thought of Surrey again. Laleham, where his aunt Susan's old house on Ferry Road was available, was one possibility. But among the other Harrow parents were the present owners of nearby Pains Hill Park, and in 1873 the family decided to rent the old bailiff's house on the edge of their estate. Vine-covered eight-bedroomed Pains Hill Cottage, which Arnold referred to as a "nutshell," would be their home for the rest of their lives—in Arnold's case, for another fifteen years, in his wife's, for about twenty-eight years. Their latest blow had been almost insupportable, yet they still had their son Richard, and two daughters, Lucy and Nelly, and knew they had to get over it somehow. Typically, living in the countryside, and working hard, were the two remedies that Arnold prescribed for himself.

Pains Hill Cottage, Arnold's "rural Grub Street"

Fortunately, he did find consolation in Cobham. Soon after arriving, he wrote to Lady de Rothschild in the Chilterns that he found the place

> beautiful—more beautiful even than the Chilterns, because it has heather and pines, while the trees of other kinds, in the valley of the Mole, where we are, are really magnificent…. We are planting and improving about our cottage as if it were our own, and we had a hundred years to live there; its great merit is that it must have had nearly one hundred years of life already, and is surrounded by great old trees….

On his earlier visits to Westhumble, he had got to know the current generation of Evelyns at Wotton, and now he describes himself proudly as having truly become, "as Evelyn is pleased to say, 'a Surrey man.'" Properly settled at last, and over the worst of his grief, he regained the energy and commitment to continue with his work, both as an educationist and as a writer. His ideas in the two spheres of action overlapped, and gave him a strong sense of mission. As an educationist, he was an early spokesman for state-aided schooling for all, and as a critic of society and literature, his priority was the education of the general public's sensibility, the deepening of its humanity. It was in these years that he published such major essays as "Wordsworth" (1879), "The Study of Poetry" (1880), and "Literature and Science" (1882).

His lovely surroundings at Cobham did more than console him. He himself noted that reading Wordsworth for a selection of his poetry made him "feel more keenly than usual the beauty of the common incidents of the natural year." But, equally, his own response to nature helped him to evaluate the poems better. For example, in his introductory essay he takes issue with Wordsworth over the idea that the child is closer to nature than the adult:

> The instinct of delight in Nature and her beauty had no doubt extraordinary strength in Wordsworth himself as a child. But to say that universally this instinct is mighty in childhood, and tends to die away afterwards, is to say what is extremely doubtful. In many people, perhaps with the majority of educated persons, the love of nature is nearly imperceptible at ten years old, but strong and operative at thirty.[6]

This hints at his own development in relation to nature, as well as being a good argument for education—and, of course, a valid criticism of Wordsworth's generalisation in the Immortality Ode. Arnold had become something of a botanist by now, as well as a great gardener, occupations which grounded him firmly in the specific, and his determination to "see the object as it really is" (another of his pet phrases) comes through in this essay as a whole.

Most important of all, Arnold's sense of beauty gave him one of the cornerstones of his philosophy. He knew as well as the Dickens of *Hard Times* that without the ability to respond to our world with our hearts, we will lose our humanity. Even today (or *especially* today, when his dark prophesies about the debasement of society seem to be coming true), no one can ignore his views in "Literature and Science," where he argues movingly for literature as a means of guiding our conduct and developing "our instinct for beauty":

> ... the great majority of mankind ... would do well, I cannot but think, to choose to be educated in humane letters rather than in the natural sciences. Letters will call out their being at more points,

will make them live more.[7]

Arnold did more than anyone to establish the tradition of liberal humanism, both in Britain and America, and until the late 1960s at least, literary critics were all more or less "Arnoldian." In the last few decades, contemporary critical theory has shifted the emphasis from the author's moral vision to the structure of the "text" or its political engagement. But T.S. Eliot's words about Arnold still ring true: even if we are no longer his "disciples," most of us do read literature for its life-enhancing quality, and can still turn to Arnold "for refreshment and for the companionship of a kindred point of view."[8]

However, there was little scope in Arnold's essays for describing the natural surroundings which warmed his heart, and made him cheerful and fun to be with. For that, we must look at his letters from Cobham. Here, his own generous humanity is fully on display. "It has been a most beautiful day," he writes to his unmarried sister Fan on 25 May 1879,

> the foliage is almost all out, and now in a day or two we shall have the May and the Chestnut blossom. I have never known the birds so rich and strong in their singing; I had two blackbirds and three thrushes running about together on the grass under my window as I was getting up yesterday morning, and a stockdove has built her nest in the leaning ivied fir-tree which you will remember, between the house and the stables.... I should like to have you here for the cowslips and the nightingales....

He wrote with perpetually fresh wonder of the beauties of his own garden—its roses, jasmine, camellia, azalea, rhododendron, marigolds, dahlias, veronica, geraniums, pampas grass, laburnum, brooms, hollies, laurels and so on. He had a kitchen garden, too, and complained if his strawberries and potatoes weren't doing well, while showing off his produce when it flourished. For example, he sent Flu to Lady Ellesmere on her St George's Hill estate with a fine Duchesse pear, and was gratified to hear that their titled neighbour (actually a Countess, the widow of Francis Egerton, the Earl of Ellesmere) planned to show it to her gardener, as proof of how much better it was than her own pears. He spread nuts on the lawn for the squirrels, made friends with a jackdaw, and fretted about the effects of high winds, frost, thaw, rain and lack of rain. His love of nature in his Surrey home remained "strong and operative" until the very end.

Arnold loved the rest of the county almost as much, taking a personal pride in its many beauties. He would walk over to the Burwood area, on the edge of Walton, finding it especially pleasant to walk the dogs there after a day in London, and revelling in the browns and golds of autumn in the ferns and chestnut trees along the Walton Road. He went boating on the Wey, walking on Box Hill again, and fishing at Wotton again. He loved Leith Hill, Ewhurst windmill, and the marvellous views from that area. In the summer of 1882, he stood as godfather to one of the Evelyn children, and wrote afterwards, "I was never so struck with the beauty of that country; the parallel foldings, of which the Wotton folding is one, running up into the greensward knot of Leith Hill, are inexhaustible in beauty." Together with Lady de Rothschild, who shared his interest in botany, he went to look over John Evelyn's old herbarium—"the plants wonderfully preserved still, and his notes to them full of matter." How lucky he was to have that opportunity!

One of Arnold's favourite trees: the only surviving cork oak (roped off and propped, to the right) at Painshill Park

On such outings, Arnold was invariably with or visiting friends, for he and Flu and their still unwed daughter Nelly were not at all "the hermit and hermitresses of the Mole" as he liked to joke. The Ellesmeres, Lady de Rothschild and the current generation of Evelyns weren't even the most exalted of his Surrey circle. He was on visiting terms with the wealthy Surrey Lovelaces, whose "fantastic" house at East Horsley left him almost at

100

a loss for words, as well it might have done, for the elderly Earl had transformed his house into an extraordinary piece of Victorian Gothic. He was also invited to nearby Claremont, which was by then the home of Prince Leopold. There he chatted to the Prince's wife, the Duchess of Albany, about schools, and dined with the most important people of the age, like Sir Richard Wallace, whose widow bequeathed his collection of paintings, fine antiques and so on to the nation—London's world-famous Wallace Collection. He invited people in his turn, offering to meet Henry James at Walton Station off the 5.25 from Waterloo: "I am bent on getting you to visit me in my rural Grub Street," he wrote. He never seems to have succeeded in this, but there were other representatives of the literary world right on his doorstep: his publisher and friend George Smith lived first in Walton, then (from 1884) in Weybridge.

All this was on top of his busy social life in London, for Arnold, like most Surrey people, was often in town. He enjoyed being at his club, the Athenaeum, and the Arnolds liked to escape part of the winter by renting a place in Belgravia again. Yet their hearts were really in Surrey now, and they looked forward eagerly to being back there in the spring: "the 1st of April when we return, will be a joyful day indeed," he wrote on 3 March 1887. Oxford couldn't tempt him any more, and he refused to stand for Professor of Poetry for a third time. The chance of being the Rector of St Andrew's University failed to draw him to Scotland, either. And when he did have to leave his home for long periods, especially on the two trips to America to give lectures and visit his daughter Lucy there—she married a lawyer whom she met on the first trip—he missed it terribly. "The kindness and goodwill of everybody is wonderful, and I cannot but be grateful for it," he wrote to Fan early in the first trip, but towards the end confessed, "the desire to be back rises sometimes into a passion." He certainly had no desire to move house again.

Although Arnold had stopped writing serious poetry, there were moments when he still felt impelled to compose verses. These do contain some references to local Surrey places. For example, in a poem called "Rome-Sickness," he writes, "I pass'd to-day o'er Walton Heath," and "I cross'd St George's Hill today," and amongst the four elegies which comprise *Last Poems* (1885) there are three poems about dead pets which show just how much he loved his familiar surroundings. One is an elegy to his beloved dachshund Geist. The dog, whose name is the German word for "spirit" or "intelligence" (as in *Zeitgeist*), was still young, only four years old, and Arnold referred to him in a letter of 3 December 1880 to his remaining son Richard as "your dear, dear little boy." Part of this sad memorial poem runs:

> Yet would we keep thee in our heart—
> Would fix our favourite on the scene,
> Nor let thee utterly depart
> And be as if thou ne'er hadst been.

....

We lay thee, close within our reach,
Here, where the grass is smooth and warm,
Between the holly and the beech,
Where oft we watch'd thy couchant form,

Asleep, yet lending half an ear
To travellers on the Portsmouth Road.
There build we thee, O guardian dear,
Mark'd with a stone, thy last abode!

"Geist's Grave" is hardly great poetry, but it provides a useful antidote to the view of Arnold as aloof and intent on edification and the dissemination of culture.

The lake at Painshill Park, where Matthew Arnold skated in winter

Arnold's own death followed not very long afterwards. When he went skating on Painshill Lake in January 1886, he mentioned in a letter to his sister, "Pains Hill Lake in snow and ice was as beautiful as ever. I got on very well, and the skating did not bring on the chest pain." But he had been having this kind of pain for around eight months, and knew exactly what it meant, since his grandfather as well as his father had died in middle age. So although he was still in his 60s, he schooled himself to think of death as "a quite natural event." A couple of years after this, he had a fatal heart attack while hurrying for a tram in Liverpool. He and his wife were going to meet their daughter Lucy, who was coming home to have her second baby. His death was put down as much to his eager anticipation as to the exertion.

Matthew Arnold was buried on 18 April 1888 in the family plot at Laleham. The people of both Cobham and Laleham had been proud of their connection with him, and came out along the route to pay their last respects to him. Arnold, with his egalitarian idea of culture, would have been pleased. But the great and the good of his day also attended his funeral, among them Robert Browning and Henry James—down to see him at last. The Dean of Westminster officiated.

Within the next few years, both Browning and Tennyson, who were much senior to him, would die too. It was the end of the great era of Victorian poetry. The two older poets were buried in Westminster Abbey, and Arnold too would be remembered there by a lifelike bust. But the quiet spot under the trees at Laleham was unquestionably the right resting place for him. Sadly, he was soon joined there by his daughter Lucy's new baby, who died within hours of his birth, about two months after her traumatic homecoming.

Like anyone else, Arnold had had his foibles. For example, he was caricatured in his own times as a bit of a dandy. But his life had been busy, productive and so blameless that his loved ones found nothing to censor in his letters but private endearments (he addressed Flu as "my extreme darling") and high spirits. Printed in full at last, his correspondence now fully discloses the engaging personality of this self-avowed "Surrey man" whose writings emphasised the value of studying the humanities, and made us appreciate anew the very meaning of that term.

Caricature of Arnold by "Spy" (Leslie Ward) in Vanity Fair, *11 November 1871 (Arnold admitted that some people did see a likeness, though only in "the figure and attitude"!)*

Notes to Chapter 5

[1] George W.E. Russell, quoted by Cecil Y. Lang, Introduction, *The Letters of Matthew Arnold*, 6 vols, Vol. I, 1829–59, Charlottesville and London: University of Virginia Press, 1996. Unless otherwise specified, all quotations are from this more recent edition, which was finally completed in 2001.

[2] Arthur Galton's note in his *Two Essays upon Matthew Arnold with Some of His Letters to the Author*, London: Ellkin Mathew, 1907, p.121.

[3] *A Literary Pilgrim in England*, London: Cape, 1928, p.74.

[4] Quoted by Oswald R. Adamson in '*Our Dear Laleham*,' Shepperton: Ian Allan, 1989, pp.59–61. The title of this local history book was inspired by Thomas Arnold's regretful journal entry on leaving Laleham for Rugby.

[5] Quoted by Ian Hamilton in *A Gift Imprisoned: The Poetic Life of Matthew Arnold*, London: Bloomsbury, 1998, p.16.

[6] "Wordsworth," *Matthew Arnold: Poetry and Prose*, edited by John Bryson, London: Rupert Hart-Davis, 1954, pp.709–10.

[7] *From* "Literature and Science," in Bryson, p.654.

[8] "Arnold and Pater," *Selected Essays*, London: Faber, 1951, p.432.

Suggested Reading

1. Poems:
   "The Forsaken Merman"
   "Dover Beach"
   "The Future"
   "The Buried Life"
   "The Scholar-Gipsy"
   "Geist's Grave"
   All these are to be found in Bryson (see note 6 above). "Lines Written in Kensington Gardens" can be found in *Matthew Arnold*, edited by Miriam Allott and Robert H. Super, Oxford: Oxford University Press, 1986.
2. Essays:
   "Wordsworth," Bryson, pp.698–714
   "From Literature and Science," Bryson, pp.642–656
3. Letters
   To Lady de Rothschild, 5 Dec. 1873 (after moving to Cobham), Vol. 4. pp.185–6.
   To his sister Fan, 25 May 1879 (about the birds in the garden, and so on),Vol.5, pp.31–3
   To his sister Fan, 29 Oct. 1886 (about the autumn colours, enclosing some maple leaves), Vol. 6, pp.219–20
   These are all in the Lang edition (see note 1 above). Unfortunately, this is a really hefty set, but Bryson's selection only includes letters of more academic interest.
4. Nicholas Murray, *A Life of Matthew Arnold*, London: Hodder and Stoughton (Sceptre paperback), 1996. This excellent biography firmly rejects the "myth" that

Arnold grew melancholy in later life: "There was no slackening of his animation and joy in living" (p.334).
5. There is an excellent guide to Arnold on the web, at <www.literaryhistory.com/19thC/ARNOLD.htm>
6. "Selected Poetry and Prose" is also available at <http://eir.library.utoronto.ca/rpo/display/poet7.html>

Places to Visit

The Arnold family plot at All Saints, Laleham

All Saints Church, Laleham, has Arnold's well-kept grave, along with those of other members of the Arnold and Buckland families. The Grade 1 listed church has a twelfth-century tower, and other points of interest, including a brass tablet commemorating Thomas Arnold in the North Aisle. The final part of this reads, "In this parish beloved by him as the home of his early labours is offered this grateful tribute of respect & admiration." Contact the vicarage for an appointment: tel. 01784 457330. Laleham is close to the M3, junction 2, or to Staines or Shepperton mainline stations from Waterloo.

Muncaster House and another twenty listed buildings, including an old granary, many "protected" trees and the seventeenth-century inn facing Ferry Lane, can all be seen on a walk around Laleham, which is a conservation area. The house is no longer vine-covered, as it appears in old pictures of it. The river is close by, and the walk up to Penton Hook Lock is very pleasant.

Pains Hill Cottage was by the Mole, near the junction of the A3 and A245. It was pulled down in 1964, to make way for new housing near the roundabout (a local remembered it as being "a funny little place," so it's a real shame that it wasn't preserved, but it did look decrepit in later photographs). Arnold is remembered there only by the name of the little cul-de-sac called Matthew Arnold Close. The great house at Painshill, often visited by Arnold when it was owned by the Leafs, can still be seen from the outside, for example by looking out from the cafeteria at the Park, but has now been divided into private apartments. For details about Painshill Park, one of England's oldest, largest and most beautiful landscape gardens, see the end of the previous chapter. It is on the A3 Portsmouth Road.

The railway came to Cobham (from Waterloo) not long before Arnold died, so it's no longer necessary to take the Guildford coach or a "fly" from Walton!

St Andrew's Church, Cobham, has a memorial to Arnold—a brass plaque near the organ. The Arnolds were very active and charitable members of the congregation, and their daughter Lucy was married there, a big event for which one or more large triumphal arches of flowers were constructed in the village. The church is open from 11am to 1pm daily, except on Mondays, though it might be wise to phone ahead to the parish office, 01932 867883. For a walk round Cobham, see <www.elmbridge-online.co.uk/cobham/>

Memorial to Arnold at St Andrew's Church, Cobham

Horsley Towers, the castle-like home of Arnold's friends, the Lovelaces, is now a conference centre. Recently refurbished like Wotton House, it has literary connections of its own, because Lord Lovelace's first wife had been Ada Byron, the poet's daughter (whose own claim to fame was in the field of computer programming). However, it was with the second Lady Lovelace that Arnold chatted about flowers and so on. He really loved that part of Surrey. Horsley Towers is reached by turning off the A246 Guildford Road into East Horsley. The gatehouses are very distinctive flint and brick structures, but it is easy to miss the narrow entrance! For viewing, see <www.initialstyle.co.uk/horsleytowers/>

The Watts Gallery, Compton, which is very picturesque and beautifully situated by the Pilgrims' Way, is well worth a visit for the portrait of Thomas Hughes, and the huge cast of Tennyson in the Sculpture Gallery. Compton is easily reached by bus or road (A3) from Guildford, which is well connected by train from Waterloo. It has variable opening times. Tel. 01483 810235.

*There is a bust of Arnold in Poet's Corner in Westminster Abbey (not the same as the one in Balliol). The Arnolds' main residence in Belgravia, where they stayed before going to Harrow, was 2 Chester Square, near the more famous Eaton Square. It has a blue plaque.

6. George Meredith and Modern Love

George Meredith, 1828–1909

Just downstream from Arnold's birthplace in Laleham is Shepperton, one of the other historic Middlesex towns which were embraced by Surrey in 1965. This is where some of the most poignant episodes in the life of another major Victorian author were played out. Like Arnold, this writer would move further into the Surrey heartland in his later years, settling on the very slopes of Box Hill and drawing other literary figures of the day to him like a magnet. He was the novelist and poet George Meredith (1828–1909).

Meredith still has his fans, but they are mostly in academe. The writer whom George Eliot and many other Victorians considered a genius has no popular following these days. This is very sad, because he is one of those select few authors whose name, like that of Dickens, at once conjures up a recognisable way of writing. Anyone who does read his work knows at once what is meant by the adjective "Meredithian," though his quirky, compacted style and flamboyant characters make a unique mixture that can never be found outside his own novels. Which, of course, is one good reason why works like *The Ordeal of Richard Feverel*, *The Adventures of Harry Richmond*, *The Egoist* and *Diana of the Crossways* ought to be read again. And perhaps they will be, because their touches of magic realism and post-modern authorial intrusions should bring them back into fashion eventually.

Another great appeal of Meredith's work is (or should be) his handling of the male-female relationship, and this has already attracted new attention. His novels are full of sparky women characters, and his controversial sonnet sequence *Modern Love* is a brilliant and searing analysis of a marriage break-up. Some of these sonnets are often anthologised, and seem much more relevant to modern readers than they could have been to the Victorians—although, human nature being what it is, many couples must have suffered similar problems then as well. The difference is that the Victorians struggled with them secretly while maintaining a respectable facade, or, as Meredith put it in Sonnet XXXV, a "wedded lie."

Meredith himself never went in for "respectability," except in one area of his life. He tried to cover up his own humble background, something which, ironically enough, had fatal consequences for the relationship which inspired *Modern Love*.

These are the facts about Meredith's early years as we now know them. He was born in Hampshire in 1828, not near the Surrey border but far south in Portsmouth, at the very end of the A3 which runs past Arnold's Cobham and all the way down to the coast. There, his father Augustus was a tailor, an outfitter for the navy. Meredith's reluctance to divulge this was natural enough in the days when social mobility was rare. Moreover, he must have found the memories of those early days unbearably painful, for his mother died when he was five, the family business failed, and his father remarried and set off to try to improve his fortunes in London. Meanwhile, he himself was consigned to relatives who had a farm in Petersfield, much closer to Surrey, but was later sent off to school in Germany for two years. There are still some puzzling gaps in his chronology, but the huge effect these big changes had on him as a boy, and even as a man, is very well documented in his fiction. In his 1870 novel *The Adventures of Harry Richmond*, for instance, the young hero yearns so desperately for his father in school that he repeats his lessons mechanically while "hunting" for him in his mind. This is in the fifth chapter, but the whole book is about his coming to terms with the absence of this shadowy, mysterious figure—who is actually sent up in smoke on the last page, like a genie being let out of the bottle.

In fact, by the time Meredith wrote that fantastic finale, the eccentric and penniless Augustus had emigrated to South Africa. However, just before making his exit, he did fulfil his parental duties in quite a conventional way. He brought his boy back from school abroad, and tried to settle him in a career. After a false start with a publisher, and another of those unexplained gaps which still trouble his biographers, the school-leaver was articled to a solicitor, Richard Charnock. Meredith never really seems to have intended to enter the legal profession, but he was more than happy to be taken up by Charnock's circle of literary friends.

He was equally happy to escape office work and city life as often as he could, by walking out through Chelsea into what was then Middlesex, and beyond that—into Surrey. Here he is at last. And how he revels in it! He seems to have adopted it at once as his "real homeland."[1] In an early poem, "Invitation to the Country!" he asks the city dweller to "Cast off the yoke of toil and smoke" and immerse himself in the pleasures of spring, birdsong particularly. Like other Surrey authors before him, he became an excellent naturalist.

Yet the nearby countryside had even more to offer Meredith than space and birdsong. Charnock and his friends had started a magazine to which the young clerk contributed, and two other contributors were Edward Peacock and his widowed sister, Mary Ellen. These were the children of the well-known satirical novelist and poet Thomas Love Peacock, who lived in Lower Halliford, now a part of Shepperton.

Peacock's house in Shepperton, as it is today

Peacock's house, still there on Walton Lane facing the green and sporting its blue plaque, sometimes played host to Peacock's friends at the weekends, and Meredith's feet must have turned that way too as he got to know Mary Ellen better. She was nearly seven years older than he was (later, he exaggerated the gap, as if to explain their incompatibility) and had a child already. But she was extremely beautiful in a wide-eyed soulful sort of way, clever and vivacious, and he fell in love with her.

Their marriage took place in August 1849, not at the little local church of St Nicholas where Peacock had once buried Mary Ellen's baby sister, but at the prestigious venue of St George's, Hanover Square, London. In other ways too the young couple got off to a flying start. Meredith had come into some money on his twenty-first birthday earlier that year, and they took a long honeymoon in Europe before returning to live in Weybridge.

This fine old Surrey town is just over the river from Shepperton, and linked to it even now by a ferry service for pedestrians—a small boat is summoned by ringing a bell for the ferryman. Mary would therefore have been able to visit her father easily. And The Limes, where Peacock had found them rooms, wasn't just convenient. It was a grand establishment, remembered now in the name of Limes Road, and nearby Lime Cottages on Church Street. Elizabeth Maceroni, the landlady, was the widow of an Italian colonel, and her other guests included the aristocratic novelist Edward Bulwer-Lytton, and the artist William Frith, among whose works were the memorable large-scale paintings of "The Railway Station," "Derby Day," and "Ramsgate Sands." Mrs Maceroni herself had two charming and talented daughters, one of whom would be the model for Meredith's musical heroine in his 1864 novel *Sandra Belloni.*

*The Thames between Weybridge and Shepperton,
with the foot ferry in mid-stream*

So far, so good. Meredith's happiness during this golden period was reflected in his *Poems* of 1851. These were brimming with young love and drenched with his delight in the Surrey countryside, with its waterfowl, wood-pigeons, rooks, mists and so on. One particular poem, "Love in a Valley," caught the public's (and even Tennyson's) attention. Here, the woman herself is so closely identified with nature that she becomes "full of all the wildness of the woodland creatures." The fast pace and rhythm of the poem also express the outpouring of a large, all-embracing passion. Meredith later destroyed as many copies of the privately printed volume as he could, and rewrote and extended "Love in a Valley." Yet the effusive *Poems* marked his debut on the literary stage. His admirer William Sharp wished "that, in his later poetry, Meredith had oftener sounded the simple and beautiful pastoral note which gave so lovely a beauty to his first volume of verse."[2]

But romantic idylls have a habit of ending, especially in the absence of funding. Meredith, any thought of a legal career behind him, was trying to live by the pen, and not making much of a hand at it yet. Quite early on, too, Mary Ellen was upset to discover that the romantic yarn her husband had spun her, of being descended from ancient Welsh nobility, was just that—a yarn.[3] By the time of the 1851 census, Meredith was staying in more ordinary accommodation behind the High Street (now 54/56 Baker Street), while Mary was in Shepperton again with her father.

Vine Cottage, Shepperton

The marriage limped on for several years, producing one son, Arthur, who was born at Peacock's house in 1853. Soon afterwards, the young family moved (or perhaps were persuaded to move) into Vine Cottage on Russell Road, a couple of minutes' walk away across the green. The pretty vine-covered cottage still stands, and it's easy to imagine the comings and goings between the two homes. At this time, Mary thought up a scheme to add to the family income by running a servant-girls' school. It came to nothing, but it does suggest the strain the marriage was under.

There had, in fact, been an accumulation of problems. To take only the worst, before baby Arthur there had been two stillbirths, and in 1851 Mary had also lost her mother, who had never got over the death of her second little girl in 1826 (for whom Peacock had composed a touching elegy). A highly-strung, passionate woman herself, Mary seems to have found the strain of these years all too much for her. Catherine Horne, wife of the Victorian editor and adventurer Richard Hengist Horne, spent three weeks with the Merediths in the late autumn of 1852, and sent her husband a startling account of one of the couple's quarrels, during which Mary screamed loudly and (Catherine suspected) was ready to "throw herself in the river," only to dress for Sunday dinner with her father afterwards as if nothing had happened. "What a strange nature he must have to bear this, and still retain his affection for her," she said, adding, "How will it end?"[4]

The marriage finally broke down completely in 1857, when Mary ran off with the painter Henry Wallis, who had recently used Meredith as a model for his most famous painting, his portrayal of the tragic young eighteenth-century poet Chatterton. One of Meredith's biographers has claimed that Mary never loved Wallis,[5] but a letter she sent him at that time suggests that she felt far more for him than she had ever felt for Meredith—more, perhaps, than Meredith had once felt for her. "I am always dreading to lose you because I feel I have no right to you," she wrote to Wallis, "and I love you so really, so far beyond anything I have known of love." She looks soulfully at the artist in his pencil portrait of her of 1858.

Mary Ellen Meredith. Pencil portrait by Henry Wallis

With this long-drawn-out tragedy as its material, Meredith's new love poetry was quite different from that contained in the youthful *Poems*. Although he was now making a name for himself as a novelist, his sonnet cycle of 1862, *Modern Love*, is probably the most enduring of his works. Inevitably, since it drew so heavily on his own experience, it was considered immoral, and sold badly at first. But after a while, it was accepted and indeed greatly admired.

The fifty sonnets follow the ebb and flow of feelings in a fraught marriage, in which a wife feels neglected and turns elsewhere for love, and the betrayed husband distracts himself with a new love of his own. Silence falls between them, and the chain on it merely "clanks" as the man makes banal responses to his wife's tentative probings (Sonnet XXXIV). Their marriage is now a performance which cannot last, but must end in some great denouement. Yet, poignantly, in the midst of such high emotional drama, the pair can still stroll by the river together on an autumn evening, feeling momentarily at one with each other and nature:

> We saw the swallows gathering in the sky,
> And in the osier-isle we heard them noise.
> We had not to look back on summer joys,
> Or forward to a summer of bright dye:
> But in the largeness of the evening earth
> Our spirits grew as we went side by side
> The hour became her husband and my bride.
> Love, that had robbed us so, thus blessed our dearth!
> The pilgrims of the year waxed very loud
> In multitudinous chatterings, as the flood
> Full brown came from the West, and like pale blood
> Expanded to the upper crimson cloud.
> Love, that had robbed us of immortal things,
> This little moment mercifully gave,
> Where I have seen across the twilight wave
> The swan sail with her young beneath her wings.
>
> (Sonnet XLVII)

No one who has read this expansive sixteen-line sonnet can walk along the Thames at Shepperton, with its several "willow islands," without imagining the estranged couple walking there in real life, lulled into a truce by the harmony of their surroundings.

Such truces are fragile. The end comes in the sonnets when the two finally draw out each other's true feelings. In doing so, they twist the knife in each other's hearts, and in her anguish the woman decides to free her husband by committing suicide. "How piteously Love closed what he begat!" cries the despairing speaker in the last sonnet.

Like Sonnet XLVII, many key episodes in the novels of this time are set in scenes reminiscent of Meredith's local haunts. For instance, in *The Ordeal of Richard Feverel*, which was published in 1859, the impressionable young hero glimpses Lucy Desborough when boating on a stretch of river with a rushing weir, very much like that at Shepperton. Lucy's surname itself connects her strongly with the area, for the Thames at Shepperton loops round a piece of land called Desborough Island, with the narrow Desborough

Channel enclosing it from the other side. Again, the emotional moment is indissolubly linked with the place itself. "Surrounded by the green shaven meadows, the pastoral summer buzz, the weirfields thundering white, amid the breath and beauty of wild flowers, she was a bit of lovely human life in a fair setting," writes Meredith in Chapter 14. As for the heartstruck Richard, "It was the First Woman to him," says the narrator in the next chapter, summing up the paradisiacal encounter and also perhaps giving a hint of "the fall" to come. Surrey was Eden to Meredith, and it was there that he had suffered a terrible betrayal.

The Thames at Shepperton, looking across at Pharaoh's Island

Luckily, Meredith's temperament was quite different from that of the suicidal young Chatterton for whom he had modelled. Far from desponding after Mary left him, he was more active than ever. He took lodgings in Esher, first upstairs at The Grapes, an old coaching inn (now converted into offices) at the top of Esher High Street, and then at Copsham Cottage (renamed Meredith Cottage, but demolished in April 2005) on the round-about where the A3 crosses Copsem Lane. Whilst in Esher, he cultivated new friends and walked off his sorrows with them. One day, for instance, he went south to Mickleham via Dorking, and then south-west to Milford through Shere, Albury, Guildford and Godalming, a distance of at least twenty-five miles. Then, after a stopover at Milford, he and his friend continued on to Haslemere on the Surrey border. Friends came down from London, too, after Meredith had moved to Copsham Cottage and had space for them. Among them were the poet Swinburne and the Pre-Raphaelite artist Rossetti, who arrived flourishing an unknown poem which they all found enchanting. It was *The Rubáiyát of Omar Khayyám*, and between them they would spread its fame far and wide.

114

During these Esher years, Meredith even managed to fall in love again—twice. The first time was with a Weybridge girl whom he had originally met just after his marriage. Janet Duff Gordon (no doubt the distraction of the *Modern Love* sequence) was from the upper-class family at Nutfield Cottage, near The Limes. She had been a mere child then, and he had entertained her with the fanciful tales that had evolved into his first novel, *The Shaving of Shagpat*. This new/old relationship didn't last. After all, he was still legally married to Mary, and responsible for little Arthur—whom Janet often found herself looking after for him. Unsurprisingly, she ended up marrying someone else in December 1860.

However, Meredith was soon to be a respectable widower. Mary died in 1861, never having regained either her strength or spirits after the birth of her son by Wallis. Although Wallis had left her by then, and she was living close by in the Oatlands district of Weybridge, Meredith wouldn't visit her in her last illness, nor would he attend her funeral at St Nicholas Church, Shepperton, where her baby sister had been buried. It seems that he was able to work out his bitterness much better in his creative work than in real life.

On the other hand, he was clearly moving on from that fraught relationship. Three years later, he proposed to Marie Vulliamy, a calm, affectionate young woman of Huguenot extraction who was living in Mickleham with her widowed father. Meredith would never forget his first wife, who lives on in his fiery and wilful heroines. But he had found someone almost as pretty, in an unobtrusive sort of way, and much less demanding. The couple were married in September 1864 at St Michael's in Mickleham, the very same quaint little church near Box Hill where Fanny Burney had married her French general seventy years earlier.

Now Meredith could put down roots at last. And, after a period in lodgings in Kingston, he did so in the place he loved best. In 1868, the couple, together with their little boy William, moved into their life's home—Flint Cottage, just above Burford Bridge on the lower slopes of Box Hill. There, they had another child, a little girl called Mariette but known as Rietta, in 1871: "I walked to the doctor at Dorking and again—you should have seen me!—I drove his white horse for obstetric instruments" he wrote to a good friend, saying that the birth had been "a Titanic struggle." The man who had claimed before his Mickleham wedding that he had "never had sister, or brother, or family, or love," had finally made a family of his own.

Meredith adored his Box Hill home: "we live in a small cottage in very beautiful country," he informed one correspondent. Needing peace in which to work, he had a two-room chalet built at the top of the sloping garden, which he used for his writing. He often slept and ate there as well, filling it with tobacco smoke and talking freely to his characters. To another correspondent, he wrote:

I work and sleep up in my cottage at present, and anything grander than the days and nights at my porch you will not find away from the Alps; for the dark line of my hill runs up to the stars, the valley below is a soundless gulf. There I pace like a shipman before turning in. In the day, with the south-west blowing, I have a brilliant universe rolling up to me....[6]

His periods of hermit-like seclusion here may seem ironic, considering how much he had longed for domestic relationships. But Victorian men didn't expect (and weren't expected) to cut much of a figure in the house, and the arrangement suited him. In his chalet he produced some of his best work, establishing himself solidly at last in the world of letters.

A "small cottage in a very beautiful country": Flint Cottage as it is today

For public taste in England was now catching up with his novels. To some extent, he had shaped that taste himself. Since 1860 he had been the reader for the big Victorian publishers Chapman and Hall, and this meant that he selected many of the books which people read. For example, he was the first to encourage and advise the young Thomas Hardy. His theories in *An Essay on Comedy*, first given as a talk at the London Institute in 1877, also had their effect, especially when they were embodied in *The Egoist*, his witty and perceptive novel of 1879. Here, a strong heroine very like Meredith's first wife humiliates a proud and pompous tyrant who, as Meredith himself admitted, has a great deal of his author in him. The tragedy of his early manhood has been completely reworked and served up by the mature Meredith as an entertainment, and in this new form, it sparkles. One of Meredith's most appreciative readers was Oscar Wilde, who in his 1891 dialogue-essay "The Critic as Artist" accurately described Meredith as a "prose Browning"—and who would himself turn out to be a master of discomfiture and witty dialogue.

Popular success followed critical approval with the publication in 1885 of Meredith's *Diana of the Crossways*. This is based on the real-life story of

Caroline Norton, whose escape from an unhappy marriage made her a pioneer of women's rights. Caroline Norton herself had local connections. She was the granddaughter of Sheridan, who had lived nearby at Polesden Lacey. Meredith had actually met her while he was in Esher. Diana, her fictional representative, is said to come from only a little further away: Crossways is the name of the only crossroad on the A25 between Abinger Hammer and Evelyn's Wotton, and there even now, on the corner of Raikes Lane and the Guildford Road, is Crossways Farm, with its seventeenth-century double porch and brick cornices. Perhaps because Diana is such an attractive character, perhaps because of his psychological insights, and also no doubt because of the echoes of Caroline Norton's real-life struggle, Meredith struck a real chord with the public this time. The book went to three editions in as many months.

As might be expected from the author of *Modern Love* and *The Ordeal of Richard Feverel*, the Surrey setting of this acclaimed novel is much more than a mere backdrop. Chapter 19, for example, headed "A Drive in Sunlight and a Drive in Moonlight," is very much a chapter of light and shade. Diana has recently returned from the Mediterranean and is riding with her friend Emma through very familiar, well-wooded scenery:

> Through an old gravel-cutting a gateway led to the turf of the down … the dark ridge of the fir and heath country ran companionably to the South-west…. Yews, junipers, radiant beeches, and gleams of the service-tree or the white-beam spotted the semicircle of swelling green Down black and silver. The sun in the valley sharpened his beams on squares of buttercups, and made a pond a diamond.

Diana is so taken with the view that she cries, "I should like to build a hut on this point, and wait for such a day to return. It brings me to life." But the moment of typically Meredithian exhilaration is followed immediately by bad news. Lord Dannisburgh, the older man with whom she has been wrongly suspected of having an affair, has died in town. Risking her reputation even further, Diana goes to watch by his body that night, and is increasingly enveloped in the dark overtones of the plot. As she is persecuted for her independent spirit, Meredith again reveals the kind of understanding and compassion that seems to have eluded him in his relationships with real women (including, it would seem, the patient Marie).

During his later years at Box Hill, Meredith's stock rose higher and higher. He replaced Tennyson as President of the Society of Authors in 1892, and received the Order of Merit for his services to literature in 1905. As mentioned in Chapter 4 above, authors as diverse as James Barrie and Sir Arthur Conan Doyle found their way to Flint Cottage, as well as Stevenson, Henry James—and Hardy, whose career he had furthered as publisher's reader. A letter of appreciation presented to him on his 70th birthday was signed by all these literary figures, and many more.

Meredith never lost his delight in the Surrey countryside. For many years he continued to take hikes across it. His feeling about such walks appears quite dramatically at the beginning of a poem of 1888 entitled "Nature and Life":

> Leave the uproar: at a leap
> Thou shalt strike a woodland path,
> Enter silence, not of sleep,
> Under shadows, not of wrath;
> Breath which is the spirit's bath
> In the old Beginnings find....

Such pantheistic sentiments are so apt in the Box Hill area, with its truly ancient walking routes, and Meredith felt them as keenly in age as he had done in youth. The very year before he died, he wrote another poem, "Youth and Age," which makes this clear:

> Once I was part of the music I heard
>   On the boughs or sweet between earth and sky,
>   For joy of the beating of wings on high
> My heart shot into the breast of the bird.
> I hear it now and I see it fly,
>   And a life in wrinkles again is stirred;
>   My heart shoots into the breast of the bird,
> As it will for sheer love till the long last sigh.

Sadly, however, the last two decades of Meredith's life really did amount to a "long last sigh." In 1886, the year following his success with *Diana of the Crossways*, he lost his supportive wife, Marie, to cancer. And he himself was becoming more and more disabled. He suffered from the paralysing effects of a disease called *locomotor ataxia*, and by 1905, the once tireless rambler even found it difficult to get to his writing chalet, confessing that he now indulged in his "detestable habits" in the main house, filling Flint Cottage itself with his smoke and making it into a "tobacco-box." He would still send friends to look at the ancient twisted yews in Druids Grove in nearby Norbury Park, but was only able to get around such places himself in a bath chair pulled by his donkey called Picnic. Longer trips were taken by car. He also grew increasingly deaf, and perhaps in "Youth and Age" remembered rather than heard the birdsong that he loved so much.

Meredith died in the May of 1909, and, because of his religious unorthodoxy, his ashes were interred in the local cemetery at Dorking beside his wife instead of in Westminster Abbey. It was a big local event, and visiting literati were plied by autograph-hunters. J.M. Barrie was there, famous himself by then, and he was moved to write an essay entitled "Neither

Dorking Nor the Abbey," in which he imagined Meredith looking down at the large coffin which was used only for ceremonial purposes, and seeing the funny side of it. The headstone is surprisingly small but might have met with Meredith's approval. It was made in the shape of an open book displaying some favourite lines from his 1866 novel *Vittoria* (the sequel to *Sandra Bellini*):

Our life is but a little holding, lent
To do a mighty labour: we are one
With heaven and the stars when it is
    spent
To serve God's name: else die we with
    the sun.

But the only word visible now is "holding."

*Meredith's modest headstone
at Dorking cemetery*

Meredith had been a complicated man, more like the cantankerous Cobbett than either the high-minded Evelyn or the cheerful, mild-mannered Arnold, but he had often felt "one / With heaven and the stars" just living on Box Hill. And he had risen above his own insecurities to produce master-pieces of both prose and verse, which deserve a much wider readership today.

Notes to Chapter 6

[1] Ousby, Ian, *The Blue Guide to Literary Britain and Ireland*, London: A & C Black, 1990, p.309.
[2] *Selected Writings of William Sharp*, Vol. IV, *Literary Geography*, available at <www.sundown.pair.com/Sharp/WSVol_4/meredith.htm>
[3] See Nicholas A. Joukovsky's "According to Mrs Bennett" in the *Times Literary Supplement* of 8 October 2004. Meredith's claims to such a descent would have been a typical romantic flourish on his part, and it sad that they helped to destroy the marriage.
[4] Unless otherwise specified, all quotations in this chapter are from *Selected Letters*, edited by Mohammad Shaheen, London: Macmillan, 1997.
[5] David Williams, *George Meredith, His Life and Lost Love*, London: Hamish Hamilton, 1977, p.41.
[6] Quoted by Edward Thomas, *A Literary Pilgrim in England*, London: Cape, 1928, p.47.

Suggested Reading

1. George Meredith:
   The Ordeal of Richard Feverel: A History of Father and Son, ed. Edward
   Mendelson (Penguin Classics, 1999).
   The Egoist, ed Robert M. Adams (Norton Critical Editions, 1979).
   Diana of the Crossways, ed. Nikki Lee Manos (Wayne State University Press,
   2001).
   Selected Poetry <http://eir.library.utoronto.ca/rpo/display/poet221.html>
   Penguin Book of the Sonnet, ed. Phillis Levin (2001) contains three of his sonnets.
2. Elvira Casal's "George Meredith (1828–1909)—A Brief Biography"
   <www.victorianweb.org/authors/meredith/biograph.html>
3. Mervyn Jones's *The Amazing Victorian: A Life of George Meredith*, London:
   Constable, 1999.
4. J.S. L. Pulford's detailed *George and Mary Meredith in Weybridge, Shepperton
   and Esher, 1849–61* (Walton and Weybridge Local History Society, No. 27, 1989,
   available from Elmbridge Museum, Church Street, Weybridge, Surrey).

Places to Visit

Peacock House is one half of the imposing white house at the top of Walton Lane,
just inside the Shepperton boundary,
where Peacock used to live. Thomas
Love Peacock, Meredith's first father-
in-law, a close friend of Shelley as well
as being a novelist and poet of
considerable note himself, lived here
for many years. He died in 1866,
having suffered a fatal collapse after
staying among his beloved books when
a house fire threatened to destroy them.
The house is now privately owned. The
nearest station is Shepperton.

Vine Cottage on Russell Road, where the
Merediths lived for a while, is just
across the green from Peacock House.
This also looks unchanged, and is
privately owned. Meredith would have
known both the old inns on the Thames
just past the green: The Ship Inn and
The Red Lion.

St Nicholas Church, Shepperton

St Nicholas Church further along the river to the left, on Shepperton's historic Church Square. The Peacocks' baby daughter's tombstone (with the name Margaret Love Peacock and the lines of her father's sad little poem about this "blighted blossom" quite worn now) is just to the left of the church door. Erasmus, who knew the early sixteenth-century Rector, is said to haunt the rectory. Someone who visited the rectory in the flesh was George Eliot, a friend of Rev. William Russell (this was probably in August 1869 and at Christmas 1870 while staying with her future mother-in-law, Mrs Cross, in Weybridge). Russell also had a famous pupil there—James Mason Neale, the hymn-writer, who wrote or translated many of our best-lived hymns, including "Good King Wenceslas" and "Jerusalem the Golden."

St James's Church, Weybridge, at the end of the High Street, is where Meredith's son Arthur was baptised. The nearest station is Weybridge.

54/56 Baker Street, where Meredith stayed in 1851, is now partly a shop and a solicitor's office.

The Grapes, where Meredith stayed in 1859 after Mary left him, is on the A3 at the top of Esher High Street. He had rooms upstairs, overlooking the grounds of Claremont at the back. To the right is the Bear Inn, once a royal hunting lodge, and behind it is the little ancient church (St George's) where Queen Victoria worshipped on her frequent visits to Claremont. The nearest station is Esher.

Flint Cottage is a private residence in the flint and brickwork favoured by the Lovelaces at East Horsley. Meredith left it to the National Trust, but it is currently let. However, it can be seen from the road, on the right of the Zig Zag as it goes up to Box Hill. The writing chalet is also visible on the slope above it. The bank outside is nicknamed Barrie's Bank because the younger author sat there while nerving himself to meet the great man. For more details about Box Hill, see the end of Chapter 4 above.

Meredith's grave in Dorking cemetery near the Deepdene roundabout, Dorking, is very sad (I think), simply raised kerbs in the grass with a small life-size book at its head, and just his name and the word "holding" clearly visible. Turn right as you enter the gate, and it is in the enclosed space before the chapel, in the third row on the right. It is very easy to miss. However, it is the very first in the list of "Notable Graves" provided by the Mole Valley District Council for this cemetery. Members of the Atlee and Burberry family lie here as well. Nearest station, Dorking (Deepdene).

* *"The Death of Chatterton"* by Henry Wallis, for which Meredith modelled, is in Room 9 of the Tate Britain.

7. Curiouser and Curiouser: Children's Writers in Surrey

What sinister thread links one of the loveliest corners of Esher and a particularly cunning spider? Why is there a sculpture of a rabbit in Guildford, Surrey's otherwise dignified county town? Which author whose career began in Surrey could churn out a book a week, and, in her heyday, demanded initial print-runs of at least 25,000 copies? And which Surrey author's books are even more heavily borrowed from local libraries than J.K. Rowling's?

A rabbit pops down a hole at Millmead, Guildford

These questions lead us into a fascinating new area—that of children's literature. Books which come into this category express and affect the national psyche just as much as those in the loftier "mainstream," if not more so. After all, few people read Arnold and Meredith now, whereas everyone is familiar with (for example) Lewis Carroll's heroine and her adventures. The classics of children's fiction never seem to lose their hold on the imagination, featuring regularly in bookshop polls as the most popular amongst readers of all ages. Children's literature travels well, too, making this one of the most wide-ranging and eclectic of all literary categories.

Lewis Carroll himself is the most famous children's author to have been connected with Surrey. Even an Oxford don needs a home base, and for the last thirty years of his life Carroll's was the family home in Guildford, which he acquired mainly for his unmarried sisters and their Aunt Lucy, and where he stayed regularly, found ideas for his later writings, and eventually died. Hence the lively animal sculpture near the River Wey in Guildford, and the one a few feet away, of a little girl watching the rabbit as her sister reads a book.

However, Lewis Carroll (whose real name was Charles Dodgson) was neither the first nor the last major children's writer with Surrey connections. One of the earliest was Mary Howitt, and, in more recent times, Enid Blyton and Jacqueline Wilson have also been inspired by their years in the county. There have been others as well, who have achieved great popular success—sometimes while living within a stone's throw of each other.

Mary Howitt

Mary Howitt, 1799–1888

Born in Gloucester and brought up in Uttoxeter in the Midlands, Mary Howitt (1799–1888) came to live in Esher in her thirties. She may look demure and frail in her portrait, but contemporary accounts reveal that she was strong, hardworking, and active in many spheres of life. Although little of her own writing survived the "golden age" of children's literature which

123

Dodgson's Alice books initiated, she still has a solid place in its early history.

Her best-known work, "The Spider and the Fly," is the famous children's rhyme which begins,

> "Will you walk into my parlour?" said the spider to the fly,
> "'Tis the prettiest little parlour that ever you did spy.
> The way into my parlour is up a winding stair,
> And I've many curious things to show when you are there...."

This comes from her *Sketches of Natural History* of 1834. Like other children's authors of the time, Mary Howitt took the fable as her model, and blended her natural history lessons with conventional morality. So, after the fly has been lured to its inevitable fate, she adds,

> And now dear little children, who may this story read,
> To idle, silly flattering words, I pray you, ne'er give heed....

This part has been forgotten, but the opening of the spider's guileful invitation has become a part of the general lore of childhood.

It is a small enough memento of such an industrious writing career. Mary Howitt and her husband William wrote close on two hundred books between them, including collections of tales, verses, adventure stories, novels, history and natural history, translations, and numerous pieces in journals and periodicals. From 1836, after they came to live in West End Cottage in Esher (where the pleasant little road of West End Gardens is now) they were able to support their family entirely by the pen. It was from this still beautiful spot, backing onto the River Mole and bordering on farmland, that Mary produced (for example) *Tales in Verse: For the Young* and *Tales in Prose: For the Young* (both 1836), and *Hymns and Fireside Verses* (1839), while William published *The Boy's Country-Book* (1838) as well as his widely read *Rural Life of England* (1838) and *Visits to Remarkable Places* (1840). All their writing now seems symptomatic, like Cobbett's, of a nostalgia for the old ways which were then vanishing.

Yet the couple were quite up-to-date in other ways. They were, for example, very much part of the literary establishment of their day, helping to promote Keats, visiting Wordsworth in the Lake District, receiving Dickens at their Esher home,[1] numbering Mrs Browning and Tennyson among their associates, and, like Meredith, becoming involved with the Pre-Raphaelites. In particular, Mary Howitt helped and encouraged Mrs Gaskell, with the result that William was able to use extracts of Mrs Gaskell's correspondence in the second edition of *Rural Life*. In addition to her family and literary commitments, Mary supported many reforms, especially those that affected women and children. A spider's trick is simply not enough of a memorial for such a full and distinguished career.

West End today: the village pond

Luckily, at least one of her bigger enterprises bore lasting fruit. For much of their lives the Howitts were strict Quakers, and their combined interest in childhood, folklore and morality drew them to the tales of the Danish author, Hans Christian Andersen. They had left West End Cottage by now and were living in Europe, where Mary picked up enough Danish not only to read Andersen's work, but also to translate it. This is where she becomes rather a controversial figure. Some critics praise her as a pioneer, while others blame her for quietly adapting his writings to suit her own moral purposes.[2] But surely she deserves more praise than blame. Had it not been for her, Andersen's tales would have taken longer to reach the English audience, and once they did reach it, their impact was immense. They opened up new veins of bittersweet whimsy and fantasy for children's literature here, and influenced major authors throughout the rest of the nineteenth century, from Dickens to Oscar Wilde.

At this point, Surrey still had its appeal for the Howitts. After their travels in Europe, and William's trip to Australia with two of their sons to look for gold, the Howitts returned in 1866 to live just the other side of Esher, in Claygate, at a pretty house called The Orchard. It is still there at the Esher end of Hare Lane. Here, they continued to write prolifically.

However, their lives and outlooks had been changed by their travels. Surrey couldn't keep them very long. In 1870 the cosmopolitan couple returned to the continent, from then onwards dividing their year between Austria and Italy. Mary outlived her husband by nearly ten years, and died in Rome in 1888.

Charles Dodgson (Lewis Carroll)

Charles Dodgson, 1832–1898, better known as Lewis Carroll

While the Howitts were still living in Claygate, the author of the Alice books was settling his aunt and sisters not far away in Guildford. Apart from being the first children's writer to give full rein to fantasy, Dodgson (1832–1898) had a more specific debt to Howitt. By this time, he had already published *Alice's Adventures in Wonderland*, which contains a parody of "The Spider and the Fly." In the Lobster Quadrille in Chapter 10, he had imitated Howitt's rhythm, making it even more pacy, and represented the food chain by a new cast of characters, involved in a beach-dance:

> "'Will you walk a little faster?' said a whiting to a snail.
> "There's a porpoise close behind us and he's treading on my tail.
> See how eagerly the lobsters and the turtles all advance!
> They are waiting on the shingle—will you come and join the dance?"

It is all very absurd, yet, on close inspection, Howitt's spider and fly scenario has been replaced by something even more sinister. The anxious snail, the doomed whiting, the large predators and the threatening sea ahead of them—all these make up a vast, unforgettable and very uncomfortable picture of this mortal world. Dodgson had not really made "fun" of Mary Howitt's poem at all.

Indeed, some young readers and some very prominent critics have found this kind of writing positively nightmarish. Certainly, when the whiting repeats insistently, "Will you, won't you, will you, won't you, won't you join the dance?" the choice seems impossible, for *not* to join in would be to reject life, as well as death. But here is what Alice herself has to say: "If I'd been the whiting," she announces staunchly, "I'd have said to the porpoise, 'Keep back please: we don't want *you* with us!'" In other words, Howitt's warning words, "Don't be lured into danger!" have been replaced by the child heroine's own conviction, "I can stand up for myself!" With Alice as their example, most children are only too pleased to follow her from one bizarre adventure to the next, eager to take their chance in the challenging "game" of life which Dodgson lays before them.

Charles Dodgson, who understood the child's predicament and courage so well, also came to Surrey in his thirties. He was born in 1832, the very year of William Cobbett's famous acquittal, in Daresbury, Cheshire. Then he spent his later childhood in Yorkshire, at his father's Rectory in a village called Croft, before going up to Christ Church College, Oxford, in 1851. Since he went on to become a Mathematics don, he continued to make his home at the college after graduation, pursuing his lifelong interests in writing and photography alongside his teaching. But in 1868, when his father died and he moved his family to The Chestnuts, a recently built house on Castle Hill just behind Guildford Castle, he was acquiring another home for himself as well. He not only spent parts of his holidays there but also joined in local life, making friends with the banker next door and the head-master of the local Royal Grammar School. He attended church at St Mary's on Quarry Street, the oldest building in the town, and was sometimes prevailed upon to preach there.

The Chestnuts, Guildford

In many ways, Guildford was an ideal second home for him. Far from being a rural outback, the more southerly part of Surrey drew many big names in the literary world at this time. Tennyson himself, whom Dodgson had visited and photographed at his Isle of Wight residence, built a second home close to Haslemere, only a few stops away by train.[3] Another iconic Victorian figure, George Eliot, wrote some of *Middlemarch* while staying near Haslemere too, and towards the end of her life bought The Heights (now Rosslyn Court) in Witley, near Godalming. Dodgson knew her work, and it was part of the

127

contemporary literary scene against which he was reacting. George MacDonald, who rented Great Tangley Manor near Guildford in 1875, was a personal friend. In fact, the renowned Scottish author was one of those who had urged him to publish his first Alice manuscript. Another personal friend who moved nearby was Julia Huxley (née Arnold), Matthew Arnold's niece. She had been one of Dodgson's favourite child companions at Oxford. Her son Aldous would be born in Godalming, at their home called Laleham, in Dodgson's own lifetime.

For all these people, the train connections with London were a great attraction. Still better for Dodgson was the convenient journey from Oxford, involving just a change at Reading. As the eldest of four brothers as well as having seven sisters, he took his family responsibilities very seriously. Only one of his sisters ever married. The rest, apart from one who went to live in Brighton, remained in Guildford with their aunt, depending on him to look after their affairs for them. The Chestnuts was taken in his name, and he was on the electoral roll for Guildford. It was essential for him to be able to get there easily.

Guildford was also well placed for the south coast. During the vacations, Dodgson particularly liked to go down to Eastbourne. From 1877, he travelled there summer after summer for twenty-one years, taking pictures of little girls on the beach, and providing them with safety-pins so they could pin their skirts up when they paddled. The Surrey History Centre in Woking has a few of his sketches of these children, showing exactly how their flounces would be bunched up around their drawers. Such activities on the part of a now middle-aged man raised eyebrows even at the time. These days, it is even more controversial. Yet he himself was quite open and unselfconscious about it all, telling his married sister that anyone in the public eye was bound to be a target for gossip. To him, little girls just seemed to be ideal models, and also ideal partners in the various entertainments he created with numbers, letters, cards and so on.[4] It was a boon to find a rich supply of such playmates within striking distance of Guildford.

Quite apart from its strategic position, The Chestnuts in Guildford was the perfect home for the Dodgson family. It was gracious looking, Georgian in style, and with warm-coloured brick. And it was spacious, with four storeys and eight bedrooms, just the right number for his sisters and their aunt. It was also close to the town centre. When the Dodgsons had parties and gatherings, and the house itself was too full, he would stay at local inns, using The White Lion or The White Hart, both of which have been demolished now. The White Lion was where White Lion Walk is now, and The White Hart was replaced by a grocery store—Sainsbury's.

Amongst his many connections in Surrey, Dodgson's most glamorous ones were with the royal family. Prince Leopold had been a student at Christ Church, and Dodgson had been present when Queen Victoria and Prince Albert visited him at the college. Now the Oxford don was invited to his home at Claremont, mingling with the royal family and their other important guests. In fact, there was a unique link between Leopold and Dodgson. The Prince had once been deeply attracted to Alice Liddell, the youngest daughter of the Dean of Christ Church, and the original inspiration for Dodgson's famous young heroine. There had even been rumours of a possible engagement. Although Leopold had gone on to marry the blue-blooded Princess Helena of Waldeck-Pyrmont instead, he apparently still remembered his old love, for he named his only daughter Alice.

At Claremont, Dodgson set himself to amuse this Alice, just as he had once amused her namesake, teaching her and her brother some tricks with paper. As always at such gatherings, Dodgson clearly preferred the company of children to that of adults.

As for his writings during the Guildford period, the sequel to the first Alice book, *Through the Looking Glass*, was started in the very year that the Dodgson family moved to The Chestnuts. It must have been a big upheaval for such a large family, as much of a change, no doubt, as it is for Alice when she goes through the glass and finds the family pictures and so on looking very strange in the "new" room on the other side. Inevitably, some of Dodgson's experiences are reflected in the unfolding narrative.

In Chapter 3, for example, Alice's train journey to the Fourth Square can be traced to one particular journey to Guildford. Dodgson had set off from Oxford in May 1869 with a girl called Isabel who was going to London, and he mistakenly kept her ticket with him when he changed at Reading. He wrote at once to apologise.

"In another moment Alice was through the glass": the Alice statue in Guildford Castle's grounds

Words cannot tell how horrified, terrified, petrified (everything ending with "fied," including all my sisters here saying "fie!" when they heard it) I was when I found out that I had carried off your ticket to Guildford.... I hardly dare ask what happened at Paddington....

Pretending to fear that Isabel might have been sent to prison, he promises to try his best to get her out, adding, "at any rate you shan't be executed."[5] In the book, Alice, who also finds herself travelling without a ticket, is scrutinised by an angry Guard. He looks at her through a telescope, microscope and opera glasses, before announcing that she is travelling the wrong way. Her unusual fellow-passengers (they include a goat and a horse), then make some extraordinary suggestions—she should go back as luggage, draw the train herself, and so on—until the train suddenly leaves the tracks and Alice finds herself under a tree.

"All this time the Guard was looking at her":
Sir John Tenniel's illustration for the ticketless Alice

Not all the details here would have been inspired by Dodgson's fantasies about the ticketless Isabel. Others came from everyday life. Dickens himself had been involved in a derailment at Staplehurst on the South-Eastern Railway in June 1865, and the late August 1868 issues of both the *Saturday Review* and the *Illustrated London News* had carried articles about train safety. Tennyson wasn't being neurotic when he worried about his sons' train journeys to and from Haslemere. Another topical detail here is the passengers' explanation for Alice's failure to find a ticket office: "There wasn't room for one where she came from," they chorus to the Guard. "The land there is worth a thousand pounds an inch!" There speaks an author who had recently been hunting for a large family house on the new rail network!

Other "local" references in this second Alice book include those to Tennyson himself, now starting his residence at Haslemere. Dodgson's relationship with the poet had soured, and he pokes fun at him and his boys in the White Knight and the quarrelsome Tweedledum and Tweedledee. The most obvious (and irreverent) references to Tennyson himself are in the White Knight's song about Old Father Brown, an aged man

> Whose face was very like a crow,
> With eyes, like cinders, all aglow,
> Who seemed distracted with his woe,
> Who rocked his body to and fro,
> And muttered mumblingly and slow,
> As if his mouth were full of dough,
> Who snorted like a buffalo....

Tennyson liked to wear black, was dark-complexioned with dark, restless eyes, and suffered from melancholy and hay-fever. Moreover, he was known for his interminable recitations, which Dodgson, being deaf in one ear, would have found particularly hard to catch. Dodgson sent presentation copies of both the Alice books to the poet, but whether Tennyson recognised himself here isn't known!

There was a third "nonsense" work yet to come. This is the poem entitled *The Hunting of the Snark*, which is not as famous as the Alice books, but still has a cult following. It owed its inspiration entirely to Dodgson's Guildford experience. He was there in July 1874, helping to look after a sick relative, when he took a walk on the downs for a breath of fresh air. A line of nonsense came into his head: "For the Snark *was* a Boojum, you see." Once he had written it down, the rest of this strange poem began to form, developing over the next year or two into 141 four-lined stanzas in eight "Fits." These tell the story of a Barrister, Broker, Banker and other crew members whose hunting expedition ends with the disappearance of the Baker. This poor man, who had already been warned by an uncle that some Snarks are terribly dangerous "Boojums," and had fainted away when reminded of this by the Bellman, has apparently been devoured by one of them.

> In the midst of the word he was trying to say,
> In the midst of his laughter and glee,
> He had softly and suddenly vanished away—
> For the Snark *was* a Boojum, you see.

Like the Alice books, this has been taken as a spoof on Victorian society, or even as a comment on the tragic nature of human life, and the fear of non-existence.[6] Although such interpretations are disputed by those who relish the sheer verbal inventiveness of the poem, the idea for it certainly came to Dodgson at a sad time. Unfortunately, the cousin whose sickbed he was attending in Surrey did "vanish away" from tuberculosis.

It helps to see Dodgson in his Surrey setting. He wasn't, after all, simply an eccentric Oxford don with his head in the clouds. In real life, family responsibilities demanded that he set at least one foot on the solid ground of the home counties. In his writing, too, he not only played games with his child readers, but also gave plenty of scope to scholars who see dark undertows of reality beneath his phantasmagoric narratives and weird characters. Of course, all the truly great classics of children's literature can be read on different levels. Yet there's another twist to Dodgson's tale. By mixing "stuff and nonsense" in such an unpredictable way, he inspired new generations of writers as well as readers, setting the scene for the stream-of-consciousness techniques, surrealism and absurdism of the next century. The history of the modern novel might have been very different without the input of that inventive mind of his.

Dodgson died at Guildford on 14 January 1898. He was not quite sixty-six, but his health had been poor in recent years, and he had grown very thin. When he caught influenza on his Christmas visit, not even the loving care of his sisters could help him. The funeral service was held at St Mary's, and he was buried in the Mount Cemetery, where his Aunt Lucy and several of his sisters are also buried. After a period of neglect, the grave is now bright with flowers.

Dodgson's grave in The Mount Cemetery, Guildford

Thomas Anstey Guthrie (F. Anstey)

A writer who made his name by injecting doses of fantasy and humour into the often grim reality of Victorian schooling was Thomas Guthrie (1856–1934), better known by his penname of F. Anstey. Even though he only went to school in Surrey, he is included here because it was on the basis of that experience that he wrote what would become a classic children's school story—*Vice Versa: A Lesson to Fathers* (1882).

In this much-loved work, Paul Bultitude, a pompous well-to-do city gentleman, unwittingly makes a wish on Uncle Marmaduke's "garudâ stone." As a result, he has to change places with his son Dick, and endure the indignity of being a pupil at "Crichton House" in "Market Rodwell." Crichton House, as Anstey describes it, is a typical small boarding school of those times, run in a private house within walking distance of what is recognisably Surbiton station, with its "covered bridge," "break-neck" stairs and railed off space outside for conveyances (including fly-horses in those days!). The episodes at the station in Chapters 4 and 16 are fun to read if you know the station now.

The school is run by the fiery, ranting Mr Grimstone, and neither he nor his boys (nor, come to that, his pretty daughter Dulcie) are in any mood to put up with "Dick's" new arrogance and priggishness. He is harangued, flicked with towels, and generally made miserable. It is a tale to delight the hearts of all children whose parents seem unsympathetic to their sufferings, though it's quite clear too that the real Dick is not yet ready for the adult world, and the pair are both happy to swop roles again after just one week.

The actual school which Guthrie attended was run by Samuel Wesley Bradnack, who had previously lived at the large house called Pyports on Downside Bridge Road, Cobham. Bradnack and his wife Juliana later turn up in Folkestone, Kent, where again he is listed as principal of a school in the 1881 census. Guthrie doesn't identify either him or his Surbiton school in his autobiography, *A Long Retrospect*, and makes a point of not complaining too much about his life there. However, he does say that when he moved on to King's College School in the Strand, "it was a heavenly change" (Chapter 3). Perhaps that tells us all we need to know about the Surbiton establishment and its methods, beyond the fact that Bradnack's gifted ex-pupil was inspired to start this story about it while he was a student at Cambridge.

Anstey went on to become a full-time writer, and was on the staff of *Punch* for many years. But he never again achieved the same order of success. Still, thanks to regular TV and film adaptations, the school at Surbiton continues to feature in many a child's imagination of what school was like in Victorian times—tough on a sensitive boy, but quite fun really if you didn't mind the odd "swishing"!

Arthur Edmeades Bestall

There must be something in the air around Surbiton, for here lived several other immensely popular figures in children's literature. Also born in the Victorian period, although much closer to the end of it, was Alfred Bestall (1892–1986). Like Guthrie, he was connected with *Punch*, but as an illustrator rather than a writer. Nevertheless, he wrote too, for in 1935 he took over the Rupert Bear cartoon strip for the *Daily Express*, preparing the stories as well as the frames for it, and making it even more popular than it already was. A bachelor like Guthrie, he was a shy and kindly man who found a natural home for his talents in this little character, who is good without being priggish, and whose adventures always end happily. Bestall lived in Surbiton for sixty years, continuing to write his stories and draw his pictures until a few years before his death. One of the distinctive features of the Rupert stories is that the story-line is accompanied by a version in verse – the work of various hands, according to his goddaughter Caroline Bott. Bestall's humanitarianism is still remembered in his hometown, where the Surbiton Rotary Club has erected an attractive memorial to him in the children's section of Surbiton Library (see p.140). Rupert Bear fans, and collectors of the famous Annuals, might like to hunt for some local scenery in his strips!

Enid Blyton

Not far away, in Hook Road, Hook, yet another much-loved children's author first found her inspiration. This was Enid Blyton (1897–1968), the creator of Noddy and author of several famous sequences of books for school-age children, such as the Famous Five, Secret Seven and Malory Towers books. So fabulously successful and prolific was Blyton that her demands of 25,000-plus print-runs were perfectly reasonable and acceptable, but her reputation, if not her popularity, has suffered some setbacks in our own age.

Enid Blyton was always very much a "south-east" person. Born in East Dulwich and brought up in Kent, she studied to be a kindergarten teacher, and it was to 207 Hook Road that she came to take up her second job as a governess to four little boys.[7] This big house on the outskirts of Surbiton, on the left just past the Hook Underpass of the A3, was a medical practice when I first went to see it a few years ago. But Hook Surgery has since moved to splendid new premises, and the ground floor of the old premises has recently been let as offices. There is still a blue plaque, though, to remind us that the young Enid Blyton stayed at the address from January 1920 to April 1924—a key time in her life, which launched her as the J.K. Rowling of the last century.

True, the roots of her writing career went back further than this, to her own difficult childhood. She had been very close to her father, who loved nature and poetry and played the piano, but her parents quarrelled, and he finally left home at the beginning of her teens. Although another woman seems to have been involved, the young Enid blamed her mother for it, something that would lead to a lifelong estrangement. At the time, one way to escape from all this was to shut herself in her room and write. She won a children's poetry competition when she was fourteen. Another way to escape was to gain her independence as quickly as possible. Despite her promise as a pianist, she went in for teacher training, and after a spell in a prep school entered the service of the Thompson family in Surbiton. The four Thompson boys were soon joined by some neighbours' children, so that in all Enid Blyton had about twelve pupils during this time.

She found her new position congenial, and it changed her life. In a letter to one of the Thompson children in October 1962, she explained just how important it was: "I think it was the foundation of all my success, for I 'practised' on you, you know ... I loved you all ... It was one of the happiest times of my life when I had that little 'school.'"[8] She began to write directly to young readers, on their own level, not in any condescending way but with a real appreciation of the special qualities of a child's mind. She started her very first column in the magazine *Teachers' World*, on 4 July 1923, by comparing a child's mind to that of a genius: "A compliment to children! some will say. I think it is a compliment to genius." She praises exactly those qualities in children that many adults consider tiresome—their endless curiosity, disconcerting frankness and so on. And instead of wanting to squash these qualities, she wants to encourage them. "Is it some fault of our education," she asks, "that has not recognised the real trend of a child's mind, which is, surely, genius-ward in its simplicity and need for expression?" Before coming to Surbiton, Enid Blyton had had literally hundreds of rejections from publishers. Now that she was really able to relate to her intended audience, she began to get acceptances instead.

Her fame soon grew. Her first book, dedicated to the Thompson boys, was a small collection of poems called *Child Whispers*. It was only twenty-four pages long, but the poetry was written from a child's point of view, and was very well received. The next book was *Real Fairies*. Though it was similar in style and content, it was more than twice as long. She was getting into her stride. Besides, she was making a name for herself in her stream of contributions to *Teacher's World*. She began to have to keep accounts, and in 1923 earned well over £300, which was a great deal then. By 1924, her last year at the Thompsons, she was being asked by the publishing company Newnes to prepare her first bumper book, *The Enid Blyton Book of Fairies*. Her name meant something now. It was a selling point, as it still is. The figures are amazing. For example, two million copies of her Famous Five novels are still being bought each year, many of them in translation, in countries all over the world.

Enid Blyton left Surbiton in the April of that year. She was now preparing for her marriage to her editor at Newnes, Major Hugh Pollock. They bought a house in Kent, so that was the end of her Surrey phase.

It is doubtful, though, that she was ever quite as happy again. Even more prolific than the Howitts, she devoted herself completely to her writing. For instance, *The River of Adventure*, which is 60,000 words long, was written from the Monday to Friday of a single week! Not surprisingly, perhaps, her first marriage broke down, and when it did, at least one of her two daughters found it very hard to forgive her, just as Enid Blyton had found it impossible to forgive her own mother. History was repeating itself. She soon remarried, to a London surgeon, but then there were further problems. When Noddy, her character for younger children, appeared on the scene in the 1950s, his huge popular appeal backfired on her. Librarians judged her books to be too simply written, gender-biased, classist and racist—in other words, not politically correct. Some even refused to stock them. Worse still, her output was so huge that there were rumours that she used ghost-writers. She was very upset, and her writing suffered. She was disappointed, too, that an adult play which she wrote was never performed. Enid Blyton developed Alzheimer's disease in her 60s, and died in a Hampstead nursing home in 1968, a year after her second husband. She was 71.

Despite continuing controversy about this author's unchallenging vocabulary and style, the career that started so promisingly in Surbiton is still going strong. Questionable characters like black woolly-haired Golliwog have been edited out of the books, but the majority of her characters live on, repackaged for the contemporary market. A recent poll shows her books to have been the favourite childhood reading of today's adults, and they are still the favourite reading of many of the new generation of children. Books like *The Magic Faraway Tree*, written in 1943, undoubtedly influenced Rowling, as did Blyton's boarding-school stories. Time has shown that she knew the child's mind far better than her critics did.

***

Finally, there are still important children's writers working in Surrey today, just as there are important writers in other genres (like J.G. Ballard, the science fiction writer). The most important of all is Jacqueline Wilson, whose work is more frequently borrowed from our lending libraries than that of any other writer. And children buy as well as borrow: this author has sold twenty million books and been translated into over thirty languages. By coincidence, she lives very close to the place where Enid Blyton's career began. Once labelled in the *Guardian* (of 14 February 2004), "The pied piper of Kingston," she attended a primary school in the borough, and has lived there for many years.

Jacqueline Wilson

Wilson's Surrey isn't the elegant one of private gated roads and pretty rural lanes, or even middle-class suburbia, but the less talked-of one of vandalised council estates, tattooed mums and out-of-work dads. Her work may not reflect her own girlhood (though money was in short supply then, and her parents didn't get along well), but it certainly does reflect her down-to-earth take on life, portraying children faced with the kinds of contemporary dilemmas which many other children's writers prefer to ignore. One of her most popular novels, for instance, is *The Suitcase Kid* of 1992, in which ten-year-old Andrea finds herself wrenched from her home and shunted between her divorced parents. "When I'm with Mum, I miss Dad. When I'm with Dad, I miss Mum. Sometimes I can hardly believe that we all used to live at Mulberry Cottage together," she says.[9]

Wilson's realism is only part of the reason for her popularity. She also shows how children overcome their problems. It's peculiarly satisfying when heroines like Andrea emerge successfully from their trials, often by learning

136

from their own failures. "I've got it under control now," Andrea tells the family counsellor in the very last paragraph of *The Suitcase Kid*. She is all smiles again, with a stake in her two new families, and bolstered up by the extra love of an elderly couple whose own grandchildren are far away in Australia.

Because of its good balance between realism and hope, Jacqueline Wilson's fiction is often heavily endorsed by those at the front line of child management, in other words, by parents, teachers and counsellors. Perhaps it should be required reading for adults who complain that they have no idea "where the kids of today are coming from." Certainly, such work not only helps the older generation to understand twenty-first century, conflicted children better, but also suggests how to communicate with and support them. As in Andrea's case, this is a process which can bring unexpected rewards. The elderly couple, whose plight (those distant grandchildren) is another feature of our modern world, derive comfort in their turn from Andrea's company.

Jacqueline Wilson has won many awards for her books, and has received an OBE for her services to children's literature. Recently she has been selected as the nation's new Children's Laureate. None of which can be quite as satisfying as knowing that hundreds of thousands of girls recognise themselves in her heroines—and that, for more of them than we care to think, her work offers light at the end of some very dark tunnels.

***

In the long run, however, fantasy tends to have the edge over realistic narratives for children. Even Enid Blyton, whose adventure and school stories still captivate both boys and girls, is probably best loved for *The Enchanted Wood*, *The Magic Faraway Tree* and the other books which feature characters like Angry Pixie, Silky the Elf, and Moonface (now, these are favourites of my two older grandchildren). Such characters need very little, if any, repackaging for successive generations. And when fantasy is compellingly original, as in the case of Charles Dodgson, it finds a place among those timeless works which belong not simply to generations of children, but to the literary heritage of a nation, and even of the world as a whole.

Nevertheless, there needs to be a range of stories for children of each age to choose from, and Mary Howitt, Charles Dodgson and the other writers discussed here are just a few of those who have worked in Surrey, and helped to supply it.

Notes to Chapter 7

1 Perhaps this was during his stay at 4, Ailsa Park Villas, Twickenham, in the summer of 1838, when he was writing the last chapters of *Oliver Twist*. From the burgling expedition of Chapter 21 of this novel, it is quite clear that Dickens knew the route and area at first hand.

2 Katherine Briggs calls her "doubly distinguished" because of her famous rhyme, and her translation of Andersen (*Fairies in the English Tradition and Literature*, London: Routledge, 1967, p.179), whereas Elias Bredsdorff criticises her (*Hans Christian Andersen: The Story of His Life and Work, 1805–75*, New York, Farrar, 1994, p.333–34).

3 Although the lane to the house (Tennyson's Lane) starts in Surrey, it ends in Sussex.

4 The most worrying fact is that the mother of Alice Liddell (the inspiration for Alice) stopped her children seeing Dodgson when Alice was about eleven years old, and destroyed all his letters to her. The reason for this is unknown. Perhaps, as Dodgson entertained her and her sisters with stories, or scouted for more child-friends on the beach at Eastbourne, he was subconsciously trying to recapture his own happy childhood days. Perhaps too, as a shy man with a troublesome stutter, he was fleeing the demands of adult relationships. Whatever the underlying reason or reasons for his behaviour, there's no evidence that he ever acted improperly towards his young "girl-friends."

5 *Lewis Carroll: Looking-Glass Letters*, edited by Thomas Hinde, London: Collins and Brown, 1991, p.82.

6 See Martin Gardner, Introduction, *The Hunting of the Snark*, Harmondsworth: Penguin Classics, 1995, p.21 ff.

7 This was the very road in which Thomas Hardy and his wife Emma had started their married life in October 1874. Hardy published the two-volume edition of *Far from the Madding Crowd* from St David's Villa here (he had been publishing it in instalments since the previous December), but soon moved on to Westbourne Grove, London. From here, Hardy wrote to Messrs Townly and Bonniwell of Surbiton, asking them to "warehouse" all their worldly goods—four cases and boxes, mostly filled with books (see Florence Hardy's *Life of Thomas Hardy*, London: Studio Editions, 1994, pp. 135–6, and Mark Davison's *Hook Remembered Again*, Reigate, 2001, pp.10–16).

8 Quoted by Barbara Stoney, *Enid Blyton: The Biography*, London: Hodder, p.61.

9 *Jacqueline Wilson's Superstars:* The Suitcase Kid *and* The Lottie Project, London: Transworld (Corgi Yearling), 1993, p.31.

Suggested Reading

1. Mary Howitt's *The Spider and the Fly*, New York: Simon & Schuster, 2002.
2. The Mary Howitt website <www.maryhowitt.co.uk>
3. *The Looking Glass Letters* (see note 5 above). See especially the letters to Isabel Seymour, pp.82–4.

Seymour, pp.82–4.

4. *The Hunting of the Snark* (see note 6 above).
5. Barbara Stoney's *Enid Blyton, The Biography* (see note 8 above). Blyton's pieces for the *Teachers' World* are printed in Appendix 1, p.200 ff.
6. Sheila G. Ray's *The Blyton Phenomenon: The Controversy Surrounding the World's most Successful Children's Writer*, London: Deutsch, 1982.
7. "The Pied Piper of Kingston" article on Jacqueline Wilson was from the *Guardian* of 14 February 2004.
8. The two-novels-in-one *Superstars* book (see note 9 above) would be a good introduction to Jacqueline Wilson's work.

Places to Visit

West End, where the Howitts first lived in Esher, is a pretty and popular village. A commemorative plaque to their house there turned up many years later in Scalby, near Scarborough, where it had once stood in the garden of Mary Howitt's great-great-granddaughter (*Esher News*, 20 January 1961). Calls for the stone to be restored to Esher have not been heeded.

The Orchard, where the Howitts lived in Hare Lane, Claygate is still there, but is privately owned.

Haslemere, a lovely old market town with a good museum, is well worth visiting for its association with Tennyson and the many other writers who stayed on the Surrey borders with Hampshire and West Sussex.

The Chestnuts, the Dodgson family home in Guildford, is just behind Guildford Castle.

St Mary's Church, Guildford, is behind the High Street. It has a late Saxon tower, the oldest structure in the town, and the Victorian pulpit at which Dodgson would have stood when he preached there.

The Mount Cemetery, high up towards the Farnham Road, has Dodgson's grave, and the graves of his Aunt Lucy and several of his sisters.

Guildford Museum has a "Lewis Carroll" collection upstairs, including a number of toys played with by the Dodgson children. It also has an appealing model of Guildford station in the early twentieth century, not so long after Dodgson's time. This is at Castle Arch, a few minutes' walk from The Chestnuts. A booklet entitled *Lewis Carroll & Guildford* is available there.

Alice statues: Jean Argent's "Alice through the Looking Glass" stands in the castle grounds (through the iron gateway, near the bowling green), and Edwin Russell's sculptures based on *Alice's Adventures in Wonderland* are at Millmead just over the river, near The White House pub.

207 Hook Road, near the Hook Roundabout, where Enid Blyton once lived and worked, is unique for having the only blue plaque in Hook! (St David's Villa, where Hardy once lived, has since been demolished.)

The Cap in Hand pub on the other side of the roundabout has a little display about Blyton near the bar, with some old dust-jackets from her books etc.

Surbiton Public Library on the Ewell Road has the Bestall memorial in the children's library to the right of the main entrance.

The National Centre for Research in Children's Literature is located, appropriately enough, at the University of Surrey at Roehampton (<www.ncrcl.ac.uk>). It runs conferences and summer schools, and has a European Picture Book Collection.

*__The National Portrait Gallery__ has a good early photograph of Lewis Carroll at Oxford, taken from a student album, in Room 27.

Alfred Bestall memorial in Surbiton Library

8. On Target! HG Wells in Surrey

H.G. Wells, 1866–1946

There must have been something mesmerising about the short, slight young man with the intense blue eyes. Perhaps it was his sociable manner, or his decided opinions and the sharp, incisive way he put them across, or just his general exuberance. Whatever the reason, women were falling at his feet, as they would do even in his old age. Now, by an effort of will and sheer brilliance he was managing to overcome the disadvantages of a lower-class background and ill health. He was well on target to getting the whole reading public to fall at his feet by presenting it with a series of fantastic "scientific romances." This was H.G. Wells (1866–1946) when he lived in Woking.

Woking is just north of Guildford, at a busy junction on the South-West Trains network in Surrey. By road, it's a few miles further on the A320 towards Staines, Chertsey and London. It is not on the tourist track. After all, its Saxon monastery was built over long ago, and little remains of its

Tudor palace except parts of the moat and some fishponds. Besides, the older part of the town, "Old Woking," is tucked away at some distance from the station. There is little old-world charm about the present town centre, which developed next to the station. Visitors arriving on packed trains or in heavy traffic see nothing but rows of semi-detached houses ribboning out from a modern shopping-complex.

Still, Woking has some unexpected attractions—and even some surprises. There are good residential areas for its well-heeled commuters, pleasant open spaces like Horsell Common and Hook Heath, and (amongst the surprises) an exotic minareted building just off Oriental Road, and a unique town-centre memorial. The minarets belong to the Shah Jehan Mosque, opened in 1889, the earliest purpose-built mosque in the whole of north-western Europe, and the place where the first English translation of the Koran was produced. The memorial, of course, is "The Woking Martian" referred to in my preface, a representation by the sculptor Michael Condron of the "walking engine of glittering metal" described in Chapter 10 of Wells's *The War of the Worlds* (1898). It was installed to mark the centenary of the novel's first edition, and it's here because, when the fledgling author dreamt it up, he was living just a few minutes' walk away.

The Woking Martian looms above the pavement in Crown Passage

Wells lived in Woking for less than two years, but the town's pride in his work is completely justified. He arrived in 1895, at a critical point in his literary and personal development, and was happier and more productive here than he had ever been before. The novels that he published, planned and/or worked on in Woking would make his name and his fortune. Among them, *The Wheels of Chance* (1896) and *The War of the Worlds* itself, draw heavily on the topography of the surrounding countryside. In fact, neither of these popular but very different kinds of books could have been written in a more appropriate place.

***

Wells's "withdrawal to Woking," as he terms it in Volume II of his autobiography,[1] was dictated partly by illness, and partly by his love life. In the last few months, he had been trudging round London in all weathers to write theatre reviews. Never robust, his health had taken a battering. He was even displaying symptoms of tuberculosis. Along with the convenience of its fast and frequent train service to and from London, Woking could offer him the fresh air he urgently needed. Moreover, his first youthful marriage to his cousin Isabel had failed, and he was living scandalously with a student from one of his science classes, the diminutive and rather fragile Amy Catherine Robbins (whom he called Jane or, more evocatively and affectionately, "Miss Bits" or even just "Bits"). Woking was just the place in which to lie low for a while.

The couple took a house called Lynton, one of those typical Woking "semis." Wells himself described it as a "small resolute semi-detached villa with a minute greenhouse in the Maybury Road facing the railway line," where, he noted cheerfully, "all night long the goods trains shunted and bumped and clattered" past their front windows. Just as he had hoped, their stay there was liberating for both of them.

Wells was hardly a stranger to the home counties. He was born in Bromley in Kent, very close to the borders of both London and Surrey, and had spent most of his life so far in the south-east of England. But, as a whey-faced child of the suburbs, then a hard-driven draper's apprentice, he had had little chance to get out and about in the countryside. In his earlier twenties, studying in London for a science degree, working as a teacher and trying to get a foothold in the

A "small resolute semi-detached villa": H.G. Wells's house in Woking as it is now

literary world, he had been even more restricted. Now that he was a full-time writer with some publications under his belt (including *The Time Machine*, which had been serialised and was due to appear in book form that spring), and with Jane at his side, he began to make up for lost time.

In Woking, the opportunities for open-air pursuits lay right on his doorstep:

Close at hand in those days was a pretty and rarely used canal amidst pine woods, a weedy canal beset with loosestrife, spirea, forget-me-nots and yellow water lilies, on which one could be happy for hours in a hired canoe, and in all directions stretched open and undeveloped heathland, so that we could walk and presently learn to ride bicycles and restore our broken contact with the open air.

The canal in question is the Basingstoke Canal, which has recently been the subject of a preservation project, like Jefferies' Hogsmill in Surbiton. So it's still possible to enjoy the pines and wild flowers along the towpath, or to hire a boat on it, just as Wells and "Miss Bits" once did.

Cycling, however, was an art which Wells took some time to master. In those days, he reminds us, bikes could not freewheel, and the brakes were poor. In Chapter 4 of his later and much-loved novel, *Kipps* (1905), he describes the sort of emergency which could result. Here, a would-be playwright called Harry Chitterlow bumps into Kipps and sends him flying despite the most desperate efforts to stop: "I was back-pedalling for all I was worth," explains Chitterlow. "Not that I *am* worth much back-pedalling." Wells is probably recalling his own experience as a learner-cyclist. But in real life he soon became more competent than Chitterlow, and had a strange-looking tandem made with handlebars in the middle, on which he could take Jane safely all over the countryside. Quite an achievement, considering that he had to steer the bike from behind his passenger, who in one old photograph is wearing big puffed sleeves and a wide-brimmed hat!

One of his light-hearted little sketches of that time (which he called "picshuas") shows the couple setting off from Lynton bright and early on a summer's day, sheltering from the rain an hour later, out on the Aldershot road soon afterwards, at Farnham in another fifteen minutes, and finally sitting in a field beyond Alton, having a rest, before 11am. This particular trip, he says, took them eventually as far as Cornwall. That might seem a very long expedition, especially for someone with a bad chest. But, as Wells points out himself with his usual enthusiasm, it was simply the best way to travel then: "the bicycle was the swiftest thing on the roads in those days, there were as yet no automobiles, and the cyclist had a lordliness, a sense of masterful adventure, that has gone from him altogether now."

Apart from *The Time-Machine*, which had already appeared in serial form, the first novel that Wells published from Woking was *The Wheels of Chance*, a picaresque romance which is in some ways a precursor to *Kipps*. However, it is many people's favourite Wells novel, and for good reason. Amusing, charming and hopeful, it draws heavily on these early experiences in the bicycle saddle—"I rode wherever Mr Hoopdriver rode in that story," he recalled—and is quite irresistible to anyone familiar with this part of England.

Mr Hoopdriver, the hero of *The Wheels of Chance*, is very much a Wellsian figure, an apprentice draper as Wells himself had once been. Right from the start his legs are bruised from cycling mishaps, while his hands are all blistered from urgent clutching at the brake. But, with typical Wellsian high spirits, Hoopdriver sets off from his home in Putney on an ambitious cycling holiday to the south coast, at first with great difficulty, and then with more confidence. As he sails past another draper's shop in Kingston in Chapter 4, he is already glorying in his freedom. Then on he goes to Guildford, via Surbiton, Esher, and "a charming little place between Esher and Cobham, where a bridge crosses a stream"—West End surely, where the Howitts had had their first home in Surrey. Chapter 9 finds him in Guildford, where he notes the geraniums round the castle, and pays tuppence to go up the Keep of "the old bramble-bearing, fern-beset ruin," thoroughly enjoying the view across "the waves of blue upland that rose, one behind another, across the Weald, to the hazy altitudes of Hindhead and Butser" (Butser Hill is beyond Hindhead, over the border in the Hampshire South Downs). Soon, Hoopdriver is on the road again.

Guildford Castle: "the old bramble-bearing, fern-beset ruin"

On his way, Hoopdriver has various encounters, and manages to save a young woman from a "bounder." The romantic attachment finally comes to an end at Stoney Cross in the New Forest. After all, Jessie is a middle-class girl, quite above him in station. He makes his way back to Putney alone, via Basingstoke, at the end of the last chapter. However, far from being miserable, he has a great sense of new possibilities—"wonderful memories and still more wonderful desires and ambitions." The whole novel is an unambiguous expression of Wells's own hopes and aspirations, along with his delight in being let loose at last in the open air amid the beauties of nature. The delight is unaffected and infectious.

***

Indeed, this was an altogether satisfactory time for Wells. His divorce came through, and he and Jane finally got married at the end of a busy cycling autumn, on 27 October 1895. Not that the formality itself was important to him. It was undertaken largely because of social pressures. "Directly the

145

unsoundness of our position appeared, servants became impertinent and neighbours rude and strange," he complained. Still, as he himself said, "We lived very happily and industriously in the Woking home." He explains that they were quite isolated there, and that helped. There was no one else for either of them to turn to when they had some difference of opinion. One of his funny little "picshuas" from this period shows "Bits as she *finks* she is" (floating radiantly like an angel), and the common facts of the case on the other side, as she carries out her daily activities, including watering the flowers. Nevertheless, he writes in the middle of the realistic sketches that she is "really a very dear Bits indeed."

The married life that started in Woking was profoundly important to Wells's happiness and success in life. Jane would later bear him two sons, and she would always be essential to him even though he had other affairs. He wrote later, at the end of the first volume of his autobiography, that she was "the moral background of half my life." Indeed, Anthony West, Wells's natural son by one of his "other women," Rebecca West, wrote that his father "had to have Jane as the balance wheel of his existence."[2] When she fell ill with cancer in 1927, she was living alone in London but wrote to tell her husband. He hurried to her, stayed with her till the end, and was so grief-stricken at the funeral that the ceremony became an ordeal for his fellow-mourners. Another biography provides the last word on the marriage, admitting that it "had failed long ago, in the conventional sense. And yet, in a different sense, it had succeeded, and survived to the end."[3]

***

In 1895, literary success was now just around the corner. *The War of the Worlds*, also begun and mostly written to the sound of trains rattling past, would consolidate Wells's growing reputation and relieve him of all financial insecurities. When the Authors' Syndicate asked to see the rest of this narrative as soon as possible, he sketched one of his "picshuas" at the bottom of the letter. It is, he admits, "vain-glorious to the utmost degree." Yet there's something very touching about the image of him as a cat, proudly bearing home a sack marked £200 to his beloved "Miss Bits" after having left his long looping "tail" behind at the publisher's! Another self-congratulatory sketch shows a newspaper billboard advertising "Mr Wells's New Book," and people absolutely falling over themselves to get hold of their copies. Wells must have felt that he, like the Martians, was right on target for his conquest of the general public.

It seems incredible now that one place could have provided the perfect setting for two novels as different as *The Wheels of Chance* and *The War of the Worlds*. What could there possibly have been about this bustling, predominantly Victorian commuter town, in the flat hinterland of Surrey, to inspire such an apocalyptic vision of mass destruction?

A great deal, as it happens. And here is the biggest surprise that the newer

146

part of Woking has to offer. It concerns its Victorian origins, which are unique and rather morbid.

Long before Wells came to live here, this ordinary-looking mid-Surrey town was renowned, in fact, notorious, for its connection with death. Established by the London Necropolis and National Mausoleum Company, on what was originally Woking Common, lies the vast cemetery of Brookwood. This cemetery, which is now served by a branch line from the main junction, is the largest burial ground not only in the country, but also in the whole of Europe. It was opened by the Bishop of Winchester in 1854 to accommodate the bodies of the many thousands of Londoners who were dying in the great Victorian epidemics. Loaded funeral trains would run up and down regularly between Brookwood station and the company's terminus near Waterloo, and the cemetery became the final resting-place for close on quarter of a million people (the number has now topped this mark).

An angel presides over a grave in Brookwood Cemetery

Many of the dead are neatly sorted by occupation, sect and nationality. Actors, Zoroastrians and Latvians are among those with separate areas within the 440-acre landscaped grounds.

Wells himself found this "great camp of the dead"[4] fascinating, and even returned to the cemetery long after he had left Woking, accompanied by his much younger lover, Rebecca West. She too was impressed, so much so that she picked out a plot for herself. Her wish was honoured, and she was finally buried there in 1983, almost a century after Wells first came to Woking.

Brookwood may seem peripheral to Woking now, but the modern town really did spring from it. Much of what we think of as Woking today was built on the huge amount of excess land which the funeral company sold off for development. The original little village by the River Wey, unmentioned by earlier writers like John Evelyn, was completely marginalised as this new urban area sprouted further down the line. Of course, this sort of thing happened all over Surrey. At Shepperton, too, the town's modern high street developed near the station, leaving the old Church Square by the Thames isolated. But in Woking's case almost 2,000 acres of the land had passed through the hands of the funeral company first.

By the time Wells moved there, Woking had yet another association with death. The Cremation Society had selected the borough for its activities as well. A crematorium was built in the St John's area of Woking, where the country's first legal cremation took place in 1885. This is something which Wells himself mentions when writing about that period in his life, saying humorously that "few of our friends made more than five or six jokes about that."

Humour was one way of dealing with Woking's connection not simply with death, but, more specifically, with death by burning. Wells quickly found another. In *The War of the Worlds*, an unnamed narrator, whose circumstances are very similar to Wells's own at that time, reports on Martian cylinders which land in the sandpit area among the pines and heathers of Horsell Common and on other open spaces around Woking, and disgorge repulsive creatures from the "red planet."

"There, among some young pine-trees and furze-bushes…": the sandy area of Horsell Common, where the first Martian cylinder lands

These are observed quickly getting to work on engineering and inhabiting the kind of giant tripods commemorated in the town-centre memorial. They then sweep up through the Surrey commuter suburbs into London, devastating everything in their path with Heat-Rays and deadly vapours: the Black Smoke. By Chapter 9 of the first book, the dreadful burning with its "sharp resinous tang" has reduced the whole area around the Wellsian hero's Maybury house into "a valley of ashes," a charnel house of burnt corpses.

After that, humans can do little to halt their progress. At the end of this most fearful vision of mankind's future troubles, the Martians are suddenly laid low not by human opposition but by the humble bacteria of our earth.

Many things came together in this remarkable and groundbreaking work about alien invasion. Wells had been greatly influenced by his scientific studies, and especially by having been taught by Aldous Huxley's father, T.H. Huxley, who warned against the dangers inherent in new scientific advances. He was also reflecting the fears of a particular period in history, when people were on edge because of the growing might of Germany. Recently, too, the planet Mars had been particularly close to the earth, causing a great deal of speculation amongst people of all levels about the possibility of life on the "Red Planet." Moreover, Wells found in this subject matter the ideal vehicle for voicing his doubts about the imperialist enterprise, and its ruthless putting down of opposition. But Wells's current location, in a Surrey town famous for burial and cremation, was undoubtedly one important source of inspiration for this most macabre of novels.

"It's a cylinder—an artificial cylinder, man!"

For all its sensationalism, *The War of the Worlds* is surprisingly credible, and that was a major factor in its success. Here again, Wells's present location proved highly significant. Horsell Common itself was an ideal choice for the first landing, with its wide open sandy hollow (though the cylinder makes its own pit when it lands, rather than falling into the one already there). Later, Wells described how in 1895 he "wheeled about the district marking down suitable places and people for destruction by my Martians," and his research paid dividends. The combination of topographical accuracy with psychological insight turned out to be hugely effective in drawing in his readers. "O Realist of the Fantastic!" was how Joseph Conrad was to address Wells in a letter of 4 December 1898.

Chapter 12 in Book I, for instance, is about the "Destruction of Weybridge and Shepperton," and it describes exactly how the Wey flows into the Thames here through several separate channels, how the ferry crosses near the lock, and what Shepperton landmarks (like the top of St Nicholas Church) are visible on the Weybridge side. Within this setting, the fleeing people act just as one might expect, panicking and struggling with their precious possessions while a few soldiers stand nonchalantly watching on the Shepperton bank, without offering any help. Disbelief is easily suspended when a scene is as recognisable as this. As a result, the sudden eruption of

149

the Martians seems neither more nor less shocking to us than to the hapless victims themselves:

> Quickly, one after the other, one, two, three, four of the armoured Martians appeared, far away over the little trees, across the flat meadows that stretch towards Chertsey, and striding hurriedly along the river. Little cowled figures they seemed at first, going with a rolling motion and as fast as flying birds....
>
> At the sight of these strange, swift, and terrible creatures the crowd near the water's edge seemed to me to be for a moment horror-struck. There was no screaming or shouting, but a silence. Then a hoarse murmur and a movement of feet—a splashing from the water. A man, too frightened to drop the portmanteau he was carrying, swung round and sent me staggering with a blow from the corner of his burden. A woman thrust at me and rushed past me. I turned, with the rush of people, but I was not too terrified for thought.

This reads like a simple piece of reportage. It sweeps us along in the same current as the hero, who, having witnessed the destruction of St Nicholas' tower and the houses along where Peacock used to live, drifts in the scalding water towards Walton Bridge.

What the hero sees in the aftermath of the invasion also rings absolutely true. Walton itself, for instance, comes off lightly because its pinewoods have survived. Moreover, in comparison with the Mole and other small rivers, such woodland has provided a less friendly environment for the strange and prolific red weed that the Martians brought with them. Wells, like Cobbett and other Surrey writers before him, knew his terrain, and he used his knowledge to make even these strangest of events utterly convincing.

The War of the Worlds sets Wells alongside other Surrey writers who have attacked the "Great Wen" of London. However, there's some ambiguity here. Wells also mocks the suburban complacency of Surrey. "'Haven't you heard of the men from Mars?' the hero asks some people on his way home from Horsell Common. "'Quite enough,' said the woman over the gate. 'Thanks,' and all three of them laughed" (Book I, Chapter 7). With his usual acuteness, Wells has taken the measure of his neighbours, and he turns their smug laughter against them here. Even more pointedly, his hero tells the unnerved local curate whom he meets near Walton Bridge: "Think of what earthquakes and floods, wars and volcanoes, have done before to men! Did you think God had exempted Weybridge?" (Book I, Chapter 13).

Interestingly, the other popular "scientific romance" which Wells planned and wrote in Woking, *The Invisible Man* (1896), is set in a Sussex rather than a Surrey village (although the *West Surrey Gazette* is mentioned in Chapter 12—a slip of the pen?). Probably he decided that a more rural background was required here, especially in the comic opening chapters before Griffin, the young student hero, is "unveiled" by the nosy villagers. But perhaps, too, Wells thought that Surrey people would have been too blasé to take an interest in a stranger, however peculiar, at least until they felt their lives were under threat.

The War of the Worlds mural in the Victoria Way underpass, Woking

The now famous author wasn't ready to leave the county yet. When the couple moved from Lynton later in 1896, it was only to Worcester Park on its northern edge, just east of Surbiton.

There were several reasons for the move. Lynton had been cramped, even for just the two of them—Anthony West explains that the dining table had to be cleared for Wells to work on it. The noise of the trains was bothering him, too. Besides, with fame had come money. Wells was publishing one book after another, including the Darwinian novel which he had first drafted in London, *The Island of Dr Moreau* (1897). He could afford to rent a bigger place. The immediate explanation for the move, though, was that Jane's mother had fallen ill and needed to come to them. They had to be able to accommodate her properly.

The new place was called Heatherlea. It was another Victorian villa near a station, but Wells's improved finances were reflected in its improved status. It was detached, and stood on a good residential avenue out of earshot of the trains. The great advantage of it was that it had two large rooms downstairs, as well as what Wells called "a visitor's room." Here they could entertain, and began, as he explained, "keeping open house on Saturday afternoons which improved our knowledge of the many new friends we were making." They even had a gardener here, one day a week. This house, unfortunately, was demolished in the 1950s and there are many blocks of flats along the road now. Wells has no more to say about it, or his life there, in his autobiography. "I think I have sufficiently conveyed now the flavour

151

of my new way of life," he remarks, "and I will not go with any great particularity into the details of my history after we moved to Worcester Park."

There is, however, a description of the house and the general layout of the area, disguised as "Morningside Park," in the first chapter of a later novel, *Ann Veronica* (1909):

> There was first the Avenue, which ran in a consciously elegant curve from the railway station.... with big yellow-brick villas on either side, and then there was the Pavement, the little clump of shops about the post office, and under the railway arch was a congestion of workmen's dwellings. The road from Surbiton and Epsom ran under the arch....

He goes on to describe the new houses which were growing up near the station in terms of "a bright fungoid growth in the ditch." The Avenue is still there, as of course are the station and bridge, but the most interesting point of the description is that it shows how quickly Wells's standards were rising. He could now afford to pour scorn on cheap housing, both old and new. And well he might, because, according to one of his contemporaries, the editor and journalist Arthur Lawrence, Heatherlea was "quite an ideal home for a literary man."[5]

His whole life-style seems to have been on a different level now. It is painted in vivid detail by the pioneering stream-of-consciousness novelist Dorothy Richardson, an old school-friend of Jane's, who came to stay with them. Wells features as Hypo Wilson in *The Tunnel* (1919), Book 4 of her autobiographical *Pilgrimages*, and is pictured by Richardson's young narrator Miriam as a "little fair square man not much taller than herself, looking like a grocer's assistant with a curious, kind, confidential ... unprejudiced eye" (Chapter 6). The brown decor, Japanese prints and high-backed chairs downstairs seem oppressive to Miriam at first, and she is uneasy at having to contribute to all the clever literary talk. She comments on "Mr Wilson's" drooping moustache, his squeals, his open-mouthed guffaws, his sociability and his certainty about things. By the time she is on the train back to London, she is in two minds about ever returning. Later, however, she is jealous of their life going on there without her.... "One ought to be there every day," she thinks in Chapter 13. Dorothy Richardson too would become one of Wells's many lovers.

At Heatherlea, Wells was consolidating his fame by writing works like *The Sleeper Wakes* (first published in *The Graphic* magazine, 1898–9), and the more conventional *Love and Mr Lewisham* (1900). Yet perhaps the most exhilarating aspect of this period was, in fact, the social one. He was now on good terms with many of the literary names of his day, some of them his neighbours in Surrey. These included the elderly George Meredith and two other novelists in the Dorking area, Grant Allen (mentioned at the end of my third chapter) and George Gissing. Allen lived in Dorking from 1881 until 1893, when he moved to his final home in Hindhead, and Gissing, who had struggled up from humble beginnings like Wells himself, first came to Dorking in 1895. "I asked him to come over to us at Worcester Park," says Wells of Gissing, "and that was the beginning of a long intimacy." He declared a literary debt to Grant Allen, a Darwinist like himself, and acted as a Good Samaritan to the troubled Gissing, whom he nursed on his deathbed. Probably he owed something to each of them. Like Meredith's *Diana of the Crossways* of 1885, Gissing's *Esther Waters* (1894) and Allen's *The Woman Who Did* (1895) both helped to open the way for his own *Ann Veronica*, with its scandalous "new woman" heroine.

In time, Wells would get to know everyone there was to know in the literary world. This included two other writers with Surrey connections, Jerome K. Jerome, who set *Three Men in a Boat* along the Thames, and the young Siegfried Sassoon, whose paternal grandparents lived in Walton-on-Thames.

But that was later. Wells and "Miss Bits" didn't spend much longer in Surrey themselves. First they travelled to Italy in the spring of 1898, spending one month in Rome with Gissing, and then doing some touring by themselves. Then they went off on another cycling trip to the south coast. Here, Wells fell ill again, and was advised by the doctor not to return to Worcester Park. Instead, the couple rented a cottage right on the sea front at Sandgate in Kent. Jane went back alone to pack up their things, and Wells soon set about having a fine house built, in which they could finally raise a family. His health would pick up, and he would eventually return to London for the last sixteen years of his life, but he would never live in Surrey again. That chapter of his life was over.

By 1898 Wells was, to borrow the heading of this section of his autobiography, "Fairly Launched At Last." Success as a writer had involved homing in on other targets too. Now, as he said himself, "stability and respectability loomed straight ahead of us." There were to be more triumphs, children (both legitimate and illegitimate, including Anthony West), and various honours, although not those that a more conventional author of his stature might have won. A lifelong socialist, he would meet Lenin and Stalin—and Roosevelt too. A broadcast adaptation of *The War of the Worlds* in America in 1938 would send a whole nation diving for cover. Yet nothing would ever quite equal the thrill of those early pivotal years in Surrey, especially in Woking. As Wells himself put it at this point, "We were 'getting on.' At first it was very exciting, and then it became less marvellous."

***

Walter Allen, one of the most respected twentieth-century critics of the novel, claims that "Wells had greater genius ... than any other novelist of his time in

England."[6] He certainly had a tremendously fertile and original mind, as well as a magnetic personality. His influence has cut across boundaries of space as well as time, and he has an international following even today, particularly in the field of science fiction, of which he is considered the founding father.

As a prophet, he has no equal. Lacking Arnold's faith in religion and the power of the inner life to redeem human nature, he saw the future more in terms of science, imagining flying machines (which he termed "aeropiles"), apparatus for transmitting moving pictures (which he called a "kinetoscope") and other forms of technology. If he could have seen a twenty-first-century child hunched in front of a computer screen, shooting down enemy aircraft, he would have been entitled to say simply, "I told you so!"

The warlike implications of the scene wouldn't have escaped or puzzled him either. Despite his ebullience and positivism, his commitment to socialist ideals and his global vision, Wells foretold the problems of the modern world as well as many of its inventions. In Chapter 7 of *When the Sleeper Wakes*, his Rip-Van-Winkle hero resurfaces after two hundred years to find himself in a strange place, "unscrupulous, pleasure seeking, energetic, subtle, a world too of dire economic struggle"—a world, in short, all too like our own.

Notes to Chapter 8

[1] Unless otherwise specified, all quotations in this chapter are from Wells's disarmingly entitled *Experiment in Autobiography: Discoveries and Conclusions of a Very Ordinary Brain (since 1866)*, Volume II, London: Faber, 1984.

[2] Anthony West, *H.G. Wells, Aspects of a Life*, London: Hutchinson, 1984, p.21.

[3] Norman and Jeanne MacKenzie, *The Time Traveller: The Life of H. G. Wells*, London: Weidenfeld and Nicolson, 1973, p.354.

[4] Arthur Mee's heading in the Brookwood section of *Surrey: London's Southern Neighbour*, Hodder and Stoughton, 1938, pp.332–3.

[5] *H.G. Wells, Interviews and Recollections*, edited by J.R. Hammond, London: Macmillan, 1980, p.2.

[6] *The English Novel: A Short Critical History*, Harmondsworth: Penguin, 1991, p.314.

Suggested Reading

1. *The Wheels of Chance: A Bicycling Idyll* (with *Kipps*), London: Phoenix, 1993.
2. *The War of the Worlds*, London: Phoenix, 2004.
3. *H.G. Wells: Interviews and Recollections*, a small but fascinating volume (see note 5 above).

4. Michael Draper's *H.G. Wells* (Macmillan Modern Novelists series), London: Macmillan, 1987. This makes a good all-round introduction, though Wells's own autobiography and West's *Aspects of a Life* (see notes 1 and 2 above) are still the best sources for his life-history.
5. "The Man Who Invented Tomorrow," from James Gunn's *The Science of Science-Fiction Writing* <<u>www.ku.edu/~sfcenter/tomorrow.htm</u>>
6. *"The War of the Worlds" Cycle Tour*, a booklet by Iain Wakeford, is available from the Visitor Information Centre at the top of Crown Passage, a few steps away from the Woking Martian.

Places to Visit

141 Maybury Road, facing the train tracks about 10 minutes' walk to the right of the main station entrance, is Wells's old house in Woking. It looks very smart these days, and has a blue plaque. The Shah Jehan Mosque, which Wells imagined being damaged by Martians in Chapter 9 of *The War of the Worlds*, is on the opposite side of the tracks, reached by turning left at the back of the station and following Oriental Road almost to the end. At the very end in those days was the Oriental College, which Wells describes as being burnt down. This was previously the site of the Royal Dramatic College at Maybury, of which Dickens and Thackeray were both trustees. It is now a retail park.

Guildford Castle, which Mr Hoopdriver enjoys so much, is no longer "bramble-bearing" and" fern-beset," but surrounded by beautiful flower-gardens. It costs £2 to go into the Keep now, though!

The "Woking Martian" in Crown Passage is just off the town square next to the H.G. Wells Conference and Events Centre. The new town gate from the square features representations of heathland pines, the railway, the canal—and the head and leg of a Martian tripod. The Victoria Way underpass across the road to the common has a tiled mural depicting the Martians. Wells also features under the railway arches near the market place, and in Wetherspoons public house near the town centre, which has a fine representation of the "Invisible Man."

The Invisible Man reading a book in Woking's Wetherspoons

The Basingstoke Canal runs parallel to Maybury Road, and can be reached by turning left off the road just beyond Wells's old house, and going down the steps at Monument Bridge. It's possible to walk back to the town centre along the towpath. The restored canal is very much a wildlife preserve, with reeds and the wildflowers that Wells remembered. A good cycling route along the canal is given in *Get on Your Bikes in Surrey*, a handbook by Valerie Bennett (Berkshire: Countryside Books, 2001).

Horsell Common is on the other side of the canal, about 2 miles from the town centre. The sand-pit area in which Wells's first Martian lands is on a well-defined walking route, starting at the car-park on the A245 to Chobham, by the Six Cross-Roads roundabout. It is an amazing woodland "beach," now a habitat for rare bees and a species of wasp. The three Bronze Age Burial Mounds on the common were joined in 1917 by the first Muslim burial ground in England. The 750-acre common is popular with walkers and cyclists. In central Woking, heathland exists only in street-names like 'Heathside,' and in Woking Park, a very pleasant recreational area on the way to Old Woking.

Brookwood Cemetery can be reached from Brookwood Station, after Woking. A number of famous people are buried there, including Alfred Bestall, of Rupert Bear fame, mentioned in the previous chapter. The Brookwood Cemetery Society runs guided tours on the first Sunday of every month, and issues a booklet, "Necropolis Trails." Contact Anthony Montan (01483 232654). See also <www.tbcs.org.uk>

Worcester Park is easily accessible from London, and has an interesting history as a royal park.

* ***The National Portrait Gallery*** has an unusual portrait of Wells in Room 31. Feliks Topolski, the Polish-born Expressionist painter, has painted him in old age with a dynamic, forceful, even massive head, completely belying his physically small stature.

Note: there is no grave to visit. By his own request, Wells's ashes were scattered over the English Channel.

9. Abinger Ironist, E.M. Forster

E.M. Forster, 1879–1970

Edward Morgan Forster (1879–1970) is sometimes seen as a bit of an old maid, living quietly with his mother or in his college rooms while he mused on one of the great problems of human existence—how to connect the spiritual and the material in our lives. Yet think of him in his early forties. Already well-established as a writer, he wasn't long back from Alexandria, where he had been helping the Red Cross during World War I. He was a seasoned traveller, a member of the radical 1917 Club in Soho, and a friend of such well-known intellectuals as Virginia and Leonard Woolf and Lytton Strachey. He would soon be setting sail to India for a second time, as private secretary to the youthful Maharaja of Dewas in Madhya Pradesh, central India. And he had yet to write *A Passage to India* (1924), which many consider to be his masterpiece.

Brief accounts of Forster's long, surprisingly sociable and adventurous life may well skip over his connection with Surrey, especially since he was neither born nor died in the county. Why, then, is the standard edition of his works called the "Abinger Edition," after a small Surrey village, and why was his first book of collected articles, essays and so on (including his well-known "Notes on the English Character"), entitled *Abinger Harvest*?

***

Abinger Hammer, as it's called, is one of the most picturesque places in the Surrey downs. Only about five miles along the A25 Guildford Road from Evelyn's Wotton, it has its own unique history. It was once famous for iron-working. Even now, its best-known landmark is an unusual village clock which bears witness to the old local trade. Overhanging the road from its clock tower on a cottage, this quaint timepiece carries the legend, "For you at home I part the day / work and play twixt sleep and meals" on one side, and on the other, "By me you know how fast to go," and its hours are struck by the figure of Jack the blacksmith, wielding a hammer. Visitors used to have another, real-life, reminder of bygone days further along the road, where the village smithy still stands. But the last time I went, it

The clock at Abinger Hammer.
Pen and ink by Tim Frost

looked sadly neglected and there was neither forge nor blacksmith in evidence. Still, Abinger is a very pretty place and a popular stopover on tours of the rolling countryside around Leith Hill.

The fact is that Forster lived in Surrey for two great chunks of his life, and had a long association not only with Abinger Hammer, but also with Weybridge further north (as a certain plumber is proud to proclaim). Weybridge was his home from 1904–1925, when he was writing all his major novels, and Abinger Hammer was his home from then until 1946, a period during which he published several other books, including his important work of literary criticism, *Aspects of the Novel* (1927). *Abinger Harvest* (1936) is of special interest here, since the collection contains as its finale the programme of the Abinger Pageant, on which Forster collaborated with the composer Ralph Vaughan Williams in 1934, to raise money for the local church preservation fund. In the past, he might have mocked this kind of activity. Had a church fund-raiser remained the focus of *A Room with a View* (1908),[1] for instance, it would surely have sparked some social satire. However, the Abinger Pageant proved rewarding, and Forster and Vaughan Williams did another similar collaboration for nearby Dorking and Leith Hill, in 1938.

Forster's links with Surrey were forged before he was even born. The chain of events started with the close friendship between his formidable great-aunt Marianne Thornton and the second wife of the future Lord Farrer of the grand estate of Abinger Hall. Then, in 1867, came the next link in the chain, when Marianne got to know someone else, a young girl called Alice Clara ("Lily") Whichelo, whose art-teacher father had recently died, leaving a large family of children. Marianne made the fatherless girl her particular project, helping her to finish off her education at a school in Brighton, and putting her in the way of suitable employment. Nothing could have been more natural than that she should one day have dispatched Lily to the Abinger Hall household as a governess. It was natural enough too that Marianne's nephew Eddie Forster, a promising young architect whom Lily had already met, should have found his way there at the time. Romance blossomed—which seems to have been exactly what Marianne had wanted. The young couple got engaged in Surrey in 1876, and quickly married and settled down in London, where they started to raise a family. Thanks to a mistake on the part of the vicar, their first surviving child, who was registered at birth as Henry Morgan, was baptised as Edward Morgan Forster.

Abinger Hall in 1906

Sadly, Lily and Eddie's romantic story has an unhappy ending, with Eddie dying of consumption when his son was still in his infancy. Lily Forster was left to bring up little Morgan, as he was now known, alone, but with her mother Louisa and her many female relatives (including, of course, Forster's great-aunt Marianne) and friends hovering in the background.

Apparently to get a bit more independence for herself and the boy, Lily moved to Stevenage in Hertfordshire. Rooksnest, the comfortable house here in which Forster grew up, would be the direct inspiration for Howards End, the Wilcox family's residence in the novel of that title. It would instil in him a great love of "home," and be the yardstick against which all his future homes were measured.

However, the Surrey connection was by no means lost. In 1877, some land on the Farrer estate had been leased to Eddie's older sister Laura, much as a plot of land at nearby Norbury Park had once been leased to the d'Arblays. Before realising that her lease was for the comparatively short term of sixty years, Laura had got Eddie to design a house for her there. Originally called Laura's Lodge, it was soon re-christened West Hackhurst. Lily and her little boy, or even just the boy alone, often visited her there. In fact, it became a sort of home from home for the boy. Forster's first baby letter was from that address, taken down by dictation before he could even write. It started, "My dear mamma—I've a garden of roses and all sorts of things...."[2] Aunt Laura took an active interest in him, and even during his teens, when he was at Tonbridge School in Kent, Forster continued to go to West Hackhurst regularly.

These visits would all be grist to his mill later. For example, it was "his Aunt Laura who provided the County element in Forster's early experience," says Forster's first major biographer,[3] and he was to see class distinction as one of the biggest obstacles to "making connections" in the novels. Aunt Laura herself, then a busy, forceful woman, can be glimpsed behind characters like Mrs Turton, the bossy Collector's wife in *A Passage to India* who uses Urdu to welcome Indian guests to the ironically named Bridge Party in Chapter 5, but knows only "the imperative mood"! It was at Abinger too that Forster formed some early impressions of the literati, because his aunt knew people like George Meredith and Leslie Stephen (perhaps from their rambles to that part of the county). As for Meredith, Forster would read his work soon enough. Indeed, part of the prize money he won at Cambridge would be spent on five of his novels. He must have enjoyed them, too, for in Chapter 14 of *Howards End*, Leonard Bast tries to establish his cultural credentials by describing *The Ordeal of Richard Feverel* as "a beautiful book." However, in Chapter 41 of the same novel, Forster attributes lines from *Modern Love* to a "hard man," a curious comment on the flamboyant Meredith. Perhaps he had heard of the author's more curmudgeonly side from his aunt. At any rate, Forster's early visits to Abinger introduced him to two important areas of his future life: the kind of stuffy local community which he would often criticise in his novels, and the stimulating literary world of which he himself would one day become an important if rather uneasy part.

The Forsters left Rooksnest in 1893. It's not clear now which came first—Lily's decision to move to Kent so that her sensitive son could attend Tonbridge School as a day-boy, or the landlord's repossession of the house. But Forster believed it was the latter, and would vent his bitterness about it in Chapter 10 of *Howards End*, when Margaret Schlegel tells Mrs Wilcox that the lease on the family's London home cannot be renewed: "Landlords are horrible," she says. It would be a good ten years before the Forsters were really settled again. First came Forster's graduation from Cambridge, then the pair's grand tour of Italy, Austria, Germany and Belgium together, followed by a month's college-organised cruise to Greece for Forster alone, and another visit to Italy for both mother and son. Only then did they finally choose a place for their future residence.

Surprisingly, perhaps, it wasn't in Hertfordshire or Kent, or even Wiltshire, where Lily's good friend Maimie lived. Instead, it was in Surrey, in the small Thames-side town of Weybridge, conveniently situated both for Abinger Hammer and London. The distance to the former, which Meredith and his fellow "Sunday Tramps" would have made light work of, is about fourteen miles.

"It's quite pretty in some ways":
Forster's house at Monument Green, Weybridge

Mother and son did their best to put their own stamp on the new house, which they rented for £55 a year and eventually bought for £1,075, by changing its name. From Glendore (after mountains in Northern Ireland), number 19 Monument Green became Harnham, after either Harnham Hill or West and East Harnham, close to Salisbury. On a recent visit to Maimie, Forster had made a momentous expedition to the Iron Age hill fort near there called the Figsbury Rings—momentous because a chance encounter with a lame shepherd boy had apparently given him the inspiration for *The Longest Journey* (1907). He was to describe the landscape around there at some length in Chapter 13 of that novel, finding the very "fibres of England" united at the spot from which the Chilterns and the North and South Downs all emanate.

Still, he couldn't import his delight in the English countryside to Weybridge just by giving the house a new name. Harnham was much too suburban for his liking. It was in a row of other similar, recently built redbrick villas overlooking the small green with its monument to the Duchess of York who had died in Weybridge in 1820.

Monument Green, Weybridge, today. Watercolour by Diane Setek

There was still some undeveloped land behind them then, so Forster was able to report: "It's quite pretty in some ways, looking out behind over a wood and a field full of dropsical chickens" (the wood disappeared long ago). But he sounds half-hearted about it, reserving his biggest praise for the house's one unusual asset, "a beautiful brass bound door step.... None of our neighbours have one." It's funny to see Forster, who is usually so quick to mock pretentiousness, indulging in a bit of one-upmanship over a doorstep! But then, the neighbourhood was evidently not up to his standards in other ways besides. "England seems nasty after Italy," he wrote to his publisher in October 1908, after returning from another trip to the country that had inspired his first published novel, *Where Angels Fear to Tread* (1905). "We are going away in a few days," he added, "& I trust that Weybridge will air itself in our absence—at present it smells." Thames Water is still struggling with sewerage problems, especially during heavy rains.

In fact, Forster spent a good deal of his time "going away" from Weybridge, with its smell and the fog he had complained about in an earlier letter. This is where the "quiet, reclusive don" image of him really starts to break down. Although his father's legacy had now been added to by his great-aunt's, and he had no need of a career as such, he soon made himself useful by commuting to London to teach at the Working Men's College in Bloomsbury. Cambridge wasn't out of reach either, though that was a longer journey. When he went to lecture at Guildford, he would stay at West Hackhurst, even though Guildford is much closer to Weybridge than London. There was a further incentive to go down there now, because his good friend from Cambridge days, Bob Trevelyan, had built a house nearby at about the time that the Forsters moved to Weybridge. Then there were longer trips, including several months tutoring the writer Elizabeth von Arnim's children in Germany, his first voyage to India from October 1912 until April 1913, and his long wartime stint with the Red Cross in Alexandria, between late 1915 and early 1919.

Forster seems to have made a point of "going away" from Weybridge in his writing, too. The only novel with a similar setting is *Maurice*, in which the Halls inhabit "a comfortable villa among some pines" (Chapter 2), from which Maurice Hall later travels up to his London office on the 8.36 train. Even here, neither the river nor the heaths around Weybridge are described. This might seem surprising. After all, Forster was close to the same stretch of the Thames and the same countryside which both Arnold and Meredith had loved. Jerome K. Jerome had rowed that way too, and made much of it in his best-selling *Three Men in a Boat* (1889). Yet, as Forster explained in the preface to his *Collected Short Stories* (1947), memory, ideas and impulse were what usually guided his pen. He was more likely to write about where he *had* been, and had then pondered about, than where he was at the time of writing. In Weybridge, therefore, he drew on memories of Rooksnest, the Abinger area, and his various travels for topographical detail.

The "new stone church" at Holmbury St Mary

As a result, the English part of his real "Surrey" novel, *A Room with a View* (1908), is set not in Weybridge but near West Hackhurst. He had long thought of writing such a novel, under the provisional title of "Windy Corner," the name of the Honeychurches' family home there. The village which Forster calls Summer Street, described in Chapter 9 as having a "sloping triangular meadow" or green, with "pretty cottages" on either side, and a "new stone church, expensively simple, with a charming shingled spire" is easily identified as the village of Holmbury St Mary, a few miles further on from Abinger Hammer on the B2126 Horsham Road. The stylish parish church to which Mr Beebe has just been appointed is clearly St Mary's, designed by George Edmund Street, the same architect who designed the Law Courts in London's Strand. It is quite different from the more homely parish church in Abinger, where Forster's Aunt Laura and his mother Lily (under her proper name of Alice Clara Forster) would eventually be buried. Windy Corner itself is situated on the southern slope of Holmbury Hill, overlooking the same B2126. It may be based at least partly on Bob Trevelyan's house: "I wish you would quickly inhabit your new house," Forster had written to him in November 1904, "I want it for some people of mine." And there is a pond near the path to Holmbury Hill which is possibly the one which features so comically in Chapter 12 of the novel, in which Lucy Honeychurch's brother Freddy, Mr Beebe the vicar, and George Emerson go skinny-dipping, and Lucy, her mother and Lucy's fiancé Cecil come upon them unexpectedly.

Holmbury St. Mary, from the churchyard

This episode is central to the novel, because Forster uses the pond (which seems to have been drying up even then, and has had to be dug out again in recent years) symbolically, to connect his characters with the vitality of nature:

It was ordinary water, nor was there very much of it, and, as Freddy said, it reminded one of swimming in a salad. The three gentlemen rotated in the pool breast-high.... They began to play. Mr Beebe and Freddy splashed each other. A little deferentially, they splashed George. He was quiet; they feared they had offended him. Then all the forces of youth burst out. He smiled, flung himself at them, splashed them, ducked them, kicked them, muddied them, and drove them out of the pool....

"Gracious alive!" cried Mrs Honeychurch. "Whoever were those unfortunate people? Oh, dears, look away!"

When Freddy makes himself known to them, Mrs Honeychurch's comment is priceless: "What miserable management! Why not have a comfortable bath at home, with hot and cold laid on?" The contrast between the bathers' energy and spontaneity, and stifling Edwardian propriety, couldn't be funnier or more complete, though Mrs Honeychurch's shock is soon replaced by motherly fussing, and it's clear that Lucy will marry the Adonis (half-naked George) to whom she bows, and not the pompous Cecil.

It "reminded one of swimming in a salad":
the pond on the way to Holmbury Hill

For all its humour, the scene in which the pond becomes "a holiness, a spell, a momentary chalice for youth" stands comparison with the brief but beautiful description of seasonal change in the meadow, in the last chapter of *Howards End*. There, Margaret, now the second Mrs Wilcox, feels herself to be in harmony with the deepest and simplest rhythms of life. The little family which she has somehow cobbled together after the "racket and torture" of the past are moving forward into the future as well, and, in that novel's final triumphant words, "it'll be such a crop of hay as never!" Both these descriptions show, in their own unique ways, that Forster with his lifelong ties to rural Surrey believed as fiercely as D.H. Lawrence in the regenerative effects of contact with nature. Here was one means by which materialistic human beings could "connect" with their souls.

Yet *A Room with a View* also contains a clue to his reluctance to write purple passages about nature, or pontificate about it. In Chapter 9, it is the insufferable Cecil Vyse who rambles on about nature, saying, "I do believe that birds and trees and the sky are the most wonderful things in life"—but betraying his ignorance by referring to the "perpetual green" of the deciduous larch. Mrs Honeychurch's mouth twitches, rather as Helen and Tibby Schlegel groan "gently" when Leonard Bast says that he wants to "get back to the earth" in Chapter 14 of *Howards End*. Forster permitted himself some visionary gleams in his short stories, under the cover of fantasy, and even allowed the odd paean of praise to escape him in a novel, but on the whole he doesn't let his feeling for nature run away with him. It's not his style, any more than it was Jane Austen's. To borrow his own words from Chapter 7 of *A Room with a View*, "the great god Pan" generally gives way in his major work to "the little god Pan, who presides over social contretemps and unsuccessful picnics."[4]

While the beauties of Weybridge get no mention in Forster's work, his relative isolation in his mother's staid Edwardian household was vital to his productivity at this time. On his days at home, away from the distractions of London and Cambridge, he was able to live as a full-time writer, getting up late, writing most of the day in his study overlooking Monument Green (his own "room with a view"), and taking walks and playing the piano for relaxation. From the beginning, he was working on several novels at once, at different stages, so not only *A Room with a View* but also the final versions of all his work up to and including *A Passage to India* were produced there.

However, Forster did have some social life there, as well as in London, Cambridge and further south in Surrey. Having joined the local literary society, he gave some talks at the Weybridge Literary Institute—for instance, one on "Literature and the War" near the end of 1914. This Institute had been opened in 1873 by the Weybridge Mutual Improvement Society, and had a capacity for five hundred people, so it was a very proper place for such an event. It's now the home of the Conservative Club. Moreover, it was in Weybridge that Forster formed one of his most important relationships. Lily Forster had made friends with an ex-colonial couple, the Morisons. Sir Theodore Morison was the guardian of a dashing, well-born Indian teenager, Syed Ross Masood, who was sent to Forster for Latin lessons, in preparation for Oxford. This was a turning-point in the novelist's life.

Syed Ross Masood

By now, Masood was already very tall, broad, charming and exuberant—everything, in fact, that Forster wasn't (little Morgan had actually been nicknamed Mousie at his first school). They seem to have done little Latin, but their relationship reached the stage where the well-built Masood would "pick him up bodily and tickle him."[5] Their close friendship brought Forster great joy. And, of course, it opened his eyes to the exotic culture which was to inspire the last novel which he published in his own lifetime. When

Masood went to Ghent for his French, Forster missed him dreadfully. "Weybridge has been a different place since you ceased to inhabit it: there's no one I care for living here now," he wrote to him sadly. And when Masood finally returned to India in 1912, it was a matter of course that Forster, who was a seasoned traveller by now, would go out there to visit him.

Meanwhile, the days passed lazily and were quite unsatisfying. Here is his sketch of one such day, from his diary entry of 6 July 1912, written three months before he set sail:

Breakfast 10.30. Read papers & errands for mother till 11.30. Read over old work till lunch. Slept in garden till 3.0 or later. Learnt a few Urdu phrases, & read a few chapters of an easy book on Buddha. After tea rowed mother on the river very slowly till dinner. Then played piano slackly and talked. Now it is 9.45.—It is serious, even frightening, and joined with a shamed sense of unused strength. I don't feel to have deserved India.[6]

Here was another reason why Forster failed to find that stretch of river exhilarating, haunting or in any other way inspirational. He was simply biding his time until he could meet Masood again. His confinement at Harnham had helped to further his writing career so far. Now, the handsome young man who had relieved his boredom there would provide the impetus for a new adventure.

India completely snapped Forster out of the languid state into which he had fallen. Here were "social contretemps and unsuccessful picnics" on a vast new scale, together with an overwhelming humanity and a baffling mysticism—material, in short, for his most ambitious novel yet. He came back to Weybridge to write *A Passage to India*, completing it in 1924 after his second visit to India in the service of the Maharaja of Dewas.

As well as Masood, Forster got to know someone else with local connections, this time the war-poet, Siegfried Sassoon. Sassoon's paternal grandparents had lived at Ashley Park, a fine estate in the neighbouring town of Walton-on-Thames. The two writers first met in the autumn of 1919, and both benefited from their relationship. Forster, for example, cast himself in the role of a mentor to the younger man, urging him not to limit himself to satire. His advice seems to have been heeded: Sassoon's three semi-autobiographical volumes, starting with *Memoirs of a Fox-Hunting Man*, began to appear in 1928. Forster must have been supportive, too, when the two of them went to see Ashley Park in 1923, just before it was demolished. No one would have been more sensitive to Sassoon's feeling of being an outsider, as he looked at the ancestral home which he had never set eyes on before. For his part, it was Sassoon who introduced Forster to the 1917 Club in Soho, bringing him more firmly into the Bloomsbury "set." And, with his similar sexual orientation, Sassoon was someone with whom Forster could share his then unpublishable writings, including his homosexual novel,

Maurice.

Forster was disappointed in 1933 when he found out from the newspaper that Sassoon had got married without telling him. But long before that, there was a big change in his own life. Just weeks before *A Passage to India* was due to be published, Forster's Aunt Laura died, and left him the house at Abinger Hammer. At first, this was rather problematic. He and his mother had only recently bought Harnham outright. It was their very own, whereas there were now just thirteen years remaining on West Hackhurst's lease. Besides, he was wary of the "pseudo-feudalism" of life there, with its clear social demarcations. All this, on top of the depressing task of going through his aunt's things, a task he complained about to Sassoon. But he soon made up his mind that he and his mother should move to the old familiar place, and they did so. Lily lived the rest of her life there with him, dying in 1945 at the age of ninety.

The view from West Hackhurst

Forster now felt able to take more of a part in Surrey life. Of course, he still spent time in London. Indeed, in 1925 he took a flat in Bloomsbury for overnight stays. He also did a lot of journalism and BBC work (broadcasting regularly to India, for example), and put his humanist ideals into practice by heading the National Council for Civil Liberties. Travel abroad never lost its lure either, with a tour of South Africa in 1929, and a further trip to Europe and India. But in Abinger, living in the house designed by his own father, he got to know many local people, including nationally-known figures such as Vaughan Williams, who lived nearby at The White Gates in Dorking, and Marie Stopes, who now occupied Fanny Burney's beloved Norbury Park. The essayist and caricaturist Max Beerbohm, a friend of Oscar Wilde's, was another well-known figure in the cultural scene who settled in the Abinger area during Forster's time there.

The most notable contribution that Forster made to the community was by writing the speeches and programme notes for the Abinger Pageant in 1934. At first it seemed a bit of a chore. He had become rather ambivalent about nature by now, professing to be disillusioned with "the worship of vegetation," yet admitting: "Something in me still responds to it, and without indulging in that response I should be shallow, wretched."[7] Once he got the idea of using a character called "The Woodman" to tell the village's history, he decided to give free rein to that response here, partly by paying homage to John Evelyn. Episode IV is entitled, "The Days of John Evelyn," and starts with a subdued marriage ceremony in Puritan times. During the singing of an old metrical version of Psalm 68, however, the solitary figure of the diarist is seen riding across the stage, and at the end of the psalm the sombre atmosphere suddenly lifts. The Restoration is marked by the villagers throwing off their black cloaks to reveal more colourful clothes beneath. The scene is now set for a second, more typical country wedding. John Evelyn is shown attending the ceremony with his brother George and their two wives:

> There is another Country Dance, "Haste to the Wedding." When it is over, a gardener hands John Evelyn a small tree. He goes out to plant it in commemoration of the glad event, and you may, if you will, suppose it to be the tulip tree which stands by the Old Rectory to-day.

This is a fitting tribute to Evelyn as the author of *Sylva*, who (as a note at the beginning of the episode explains) encouraged the people of Abinger to replant the woods destroyed by the local ironworks. On this occasion, Forster does allow himself, in the persona of the Woodman, an impassioned Cobbett-like rant against modern priorities:

> Houses and bungalows, hotels, restaurants and flats, arterial roads, by-passes, petrol pumps and pylons—are these going to be England? Are these man's final triumph? ... If you want to ruin our Surrey fields and woodlands, it is easy to do, very easy, and if you want to save them, they can be saved. Look into your hearts, and look into the past, and remember that all this beauty is a gift which you can never replace, which no money can buy, which no cleverness can re-fashion....

At another local event, Forster was just a spectator. This was the Walton Regatta of 1945, towards the end of his tenure of West Hackhurst. He had gone there to see his close friend Bob Buckingham, a London policeman, rowing in the annual river festival. There's little doubt that this was a homosexual relationship, though Bob married, and later claimed to have been upset when Forster told him of his feelings.[8]

Forster was now in his later sixties. He had known West Hackhurst all his life, had lived there himself for over twenty years, and had done his bit for the Second World War by giving talks to soldiers at a nearby army camp. But with his mother's death that year, things again changed dramatically.

A new generation of Farrers, in whose family Lily had once been a governess, were proving again that landlords "are horrible." After the first lease had elapsed, they had said they would renew it only on condition that Forster sold the adjacent woods, Piney Copse, which the tree-loving writer had bought soon after moving there and had lovingly replanted with mixed species. Indeed, in 1926 he had written a funny satirical essay about the copse, entitled "My Wood," suggesting in a tongue-in-cheek way that ownership makes us proud, mean and selfish—and also complaining about people using the public footpath, gathering his few blackberries, pulling up foxgloves and so on. This was published in Part I of the *Abinger Harvest* collection, and nothing could illustrate better Forster's ironist's approach even to a patch of nature which he loved with a true passion. In the end, he had managed to hang on to the wood by offering to leave it to the National Trust when he died. Nevertheless, the lease on West Hackhurst was only renewed for his mother's remaining lifetime.

Piney Copse, Forster's wood at West Hackhurst

Naturally, tension between the Forsters and the Farrers had continued, with a quarrel almost immediately afterwards about the field which Forster rented between the house and the village. All this seems to have been partly a class war, because Forster felt uncomfortable with the old "manorial" family, and resented its hold over "his" property and land. On one occasion, he attended a meeting of Dorking landowners and wrote sarcastically about their arrogance and (his old criticism) feudalism. But there was nothing to be done. On his return from a literary conference in India in 1945, he learnt that he had to give up West Hackhurst, just as he had once had to give up his other much-loved home, Rooksnest.

He got a wonderful send-off from the villagers. The rector's wife, Mrs Meade, held a farewell party for him, at which he made a speech about defending the footpaths, and was presented with a book which almost all the villagers had put their names in. No wonder he would look back nostalgically on the close of the long "Surrey" chapter in his life.

In the event, he didn't really have to strike out anew. He was offered an honorary fellowship at King's College, Cambridge, where he had already had a three-year fellowship at the end of the twenties, and permanent rooms there. It was an unusual offer, which showed how highly he was thought of. Naturally, he accepted, but kept his living-room there as much like the drawing-room at Abinger as possible, and still went down to Surrey to put flowers on his mother's and aunt's graves, and, no doubt, to see "his" trees.

Forster continued to "connect" with the world in his own way. Like Evelyn before him, he refused a knighthood in 1949 because it didn't seem to suit him, but he did accept many honorary degrees and the major awards of the Companion of Honour (1953) and the Order of Merit (1969, on his ninetieth birthday). He collected more of his scattered prose writings, wrote a biography of his great-aunt Marianne, took several trips to Europe and two to the States, collaborated on the libretto of Benjamin Britten's *Billy Budd*, and went slowly up to the witness box on 28 October 1960, to inform the judge at the *Lady Chatterley* trial that he still considered D.H. Lawrence to be the "greatest imaginative novelist" of his generation.[9] He was then over eighty. He continued to meet his friends, and died at the great age of ninety-one at the Buckinghams' home in Coventry, with Bob's wife holding his hand as he slipped away. After a simple cremation, without any religious ceremony, his ashes were scattered over the Buckinghams' rose garden.

In truth, Forster needs no other memorial than the wonderfully humane novels which he wrote as a young man, in which people struggle to overcome the obstacles that society puts in the way of natural feelings. These novels, which have now reached a vast new audience through award-winning film adaptations, are still working on our sensibilities today.

***

As Forster himself suggests in his 1908 short story, "The Celestial Omnibus," books cannot be read by their covers. The boy who had been labelled "Mousie" had not led the life of an old maid at all. On the other hand, he had not been a Surrey gentleman of the old school, either. He didn't own or plough or even tramp across the land (except for little Piney Copse). Yet Surrey had been his base as a creative writer, and his lifelong association with West Hackhurst gave him his roots in the English countryside, and the continuity that he craved. His moving plea in the Abinger Pageant for *our* "Surrey fields and woodlands" shows just how much he valued this particular "connection."

Notes to Chapter 9

[1] See Oliver Stallybrass's introduction to the 1978 Penguin edition of the novel, p.7.

[2] *Selected Letters of E.M. Forster, Volume 1: 1879–1920*, edited by Mary Lago and P.N. Furbank, London: Collins, 1983, p.2. Unless otherwise specified, all quotations in this chapter are from this and its companion volume, *Volume II, 1921–1970*, published by Collins in 1985.

[3] P.N. Furbank, *E.M. Forster: A Life, Vol. I, The Growth of the Novelist (1879– 1914)*, London: Secker and Warburg, 1977, p.45.

[4] One can't help thinking of *Emma* and the Box Hill fiasco here, though nothing could beat the more exotic outing to the Marabar Caves in Part 2 of *A Passage to India*!

[5] Furbank's *Life, Vol. I*, p.145.

[6] Quoted in Furbank's *Life, Vol. I*, p.218.

[7] *Commonplace Book*, edited by Philip Gardner, London: Scolar Press, 1985, pp.37 and 36.

[8] As might be expected, the most recent of Forster's biographers, Nicola Beauman, makes a particular point of this, insisting on physical intimacy between them. Does it matter? See her *Morgan: A Biography of E.M. Forster*, Hodder and Stoughton, 1993.

[9] For a touching account of his words and demeanour then, see *The Trial of Lady Chatterley: Regina v. Penguin Books Limited*, edited by C.H. Rolph, A Penguin Special of 1961.

Suggested Reading

1. *A Room with a View* (see note 1 above, latest reprint, 2004), also *Early Sketches of A Room with a View*, edited by Oliver Stallybrass, London: Arnold, 1977.

2. P.N. Furbank's *E.M. Forster: A Life*, available in one volume as a Harvest/ HBJ book, 1994. This is still the standard biography.

3. Forster's *Collected Short Stories*, Harmondsworth: Penguin, 2002, especially "The Celestial Omnibus" which sets off from Surbiton for its mystery tour.

4. "Notes on the English Character" and "My Wood" in *Abinger Harvest*, New York: Harcourt, 1995.

5. The unofficial Forster website <www.musicandmeaning.com/forster/>

6. A useful website with links to e-texts, <http://bedfordstmartins.com/litlinks/fiction/forster.htm>

7. Not reading—but see the videos or DVDs of *Passage to India* (1984), *Room with a View* (1986), *Maurice* (1987), *Where Angels Fear to Tread* (1991) and *Howards End* (1992), with actors such as Peggy Ashcroft, Helen Mirren, Hugh Grant, Vanessa Redgrave and Anthony Hopkins. Sadly, the English part of *A Room with a View* was filmed in Kent.

Places to Visit

19, Monument Green, Weybridge, is diagonally opposite The Ship Hotel at the end of Weybridge High Street (reached by bus from the station). As shown by the opening paragraph of this book, it's still a private home. The area has another literary association: the eighteenth-century writer Oliver Goldsmith often used to stay with friends on nearby Monument Hill.

Abinger Hammer, with its famous overhanging clock, tea rooms, bustling farm shop and so on, is on the A25 after Wotton. Notice that, as well as its legend, the clock also has a inscription just below it explaining that it was rebuilt in 1891 by "Sir T.H. Farrer." The nearest station is Gomshall, one stop after Dorking West.

St James, off Abinger Lane, is the church where Laura and Lily Forster are buried. Take the path south across the churchyard from the church door. Laura's grave is along to the right, and Lily's ("Alice Clara Forster") at the far end.

West Hackhurst has changed greatly from the days when Forster lived there, having been modernised and enlarged. It is a bit of a way up Hackhurst Lane, beside the Abinger Arms public house. The National Trust footpath just beyond its private drive leads straight into Piney Copse. Hackhurst Lane itself leads on to the Pilgrims' Way. Ironically, Abinger Hall has been demolished.

Holmbury St Mary, the original of Summer Street in *A Room with a View*, is reached by turning left from the A25 at Abinger down the B 2126. The turning is opposite the Abinger Hammer Tea Rooms.

St Mary's Church overlooks the village and is a very striking piece of Victorian church architecture.

Holmbury Hill is on the famous 108-mile long Greensand Way for trekking through Kent and Surrey, following an ancient ridge parallel with the North Downs Way.

The pond which may have inspired Forster's nude bathing scene is a few hundred yards west of Holmbury St Mary Youth Hostel between Abinger Hammer and Holmsbury St Mary itself (going in that direction, turn right up Radnor Lane). See also Stallybrass's note to p.126 of *A Room with a View*, p.249. Apart from being muddy, the pond is now very exposed, as nearby trees have been cut down. Not a good place for modern skinny-dippers!

*The portrait of Forster in Room 31 of the National Portrait Gallery is by Dora Carrington. One of the younger members of the Bloomsbury Group, she has caught him in a delightfully reflective pose.

10. The Sword and the Quill: Surrey Writers in Times of War

Lines Written In Surrey, 1917

A sudden swirl of song in the bright sky—
　　The little lark adoring his lord the sun;
　　Across the corn the lazy ripples run;
Under the eaves, conferring drowsily,
Doves droop or amble; the agile waterfly
　　　　Wrinkles the pool: and flowers, gay and dun,
　　　　Rose, bluebell, rhododendron, one by one,
The buccaneering bees prove busily.

Ah, who would trace this tranquil loveliness
　　In verse felicitous?—no measure tells;
But gazing on her bosom, we can guess
　　Why men strike hard for England in red hells,
Falling on dreams, 'mid Death's extreme caress,
　　Of English daisies dancing in English dells.

George Herbert Clarke[1]

No place on earth can be rich in history without having seen its share of conflict. Surrey has always been a sought-after place to live. In the past, that could be a matter of life and death rather than high house prices. Its strategic importance, between the south coast and the capital, also made Surrey vulnerable to attack. Yet, as befits this county of ancient oaks, dappled meadows and tranquil streams, this has generally been more a place to fight for than to fight in.

The blood that was spilt here in battles was spilt centuries ago. Walton-on-Thames, for instance, where I live, and where Forster and Sassoon once walked so companionably together, is still thought by some to have been crossed by Julius Caesar and his men in 54BC, en route from the channel to St Albans. The Thames could then be forded close to Walton Bridge. The town itself seems to have taken its name from its Celtic inhabitants, who were later driven out by the Anglo-Saxons—in the Domesday Book its name is spelt "Waletona," rather more reminiscent of "The town of the Welsh (or Britons)" than the present spelling. Another snippet of information from the

Domesday Book is that the biggest landlord in Chobham, on the opposite side of Woking to Cobham, was someone called Odin, presumably of Scandinavian origin, and this reminds us of the ninth- and tenth-century Viking raids on nearby Chertsey Abbey and Staines. According to *The Anglo-Saxon Chronicle*, the raid on Staines in 993 involved 93 ships, and it's easy to imagine some of the raiders jumping ship and staking claims inland from the Thames. There is a smattering of such names among the Surrey landlords of this time.

The Domesday Book itself was compiled at William the Conqueror's command, and Surrey's value and strategic importance is best shown by its Norman castles. Guildford Castle, for example, is a fine specimen of Norman military architecture, though, like Reigate castle to the east, it was never really the scene of battle. Along with Farnham Castle, these were both briefly occupied by the French Dauphin during the first Barons' War of the thirteenth century, after King John failed to honour the Magna Carta sealed at Runnymede. But the Dauphin was here at the invitation of the English barons themselves, and would have met little resistance.

The Gatehouse of Farnham Castle today

Farnham Castle, however, where Cobbett would one day work as a garden boy, saw more dramatic action—its main gate was blown up in the early seventeenth century, during the English Civil War.

175

George Wither and John Denham

It was here at Farnham that the sword and the pen (or rather, the quill) crossed most violently in Surrey. A certain Major George Wither was appointed governor of the castle by the parliament, but in November 1642 he had to retreat in the face of the Royalist threat. A band of Surrey men under the command of the young Sheriff of Surrey, John Denham, marched in the very next day to occupy it. It so happened that Wither (1588–1667) and Denham (1615–1669) were both well-known poets.

George Wither, 1588–1667

Wither's contribution to the national consciousness is just one line. It comes from his "Christmas Carol," and, ironically (considering that he was such a staunch Puritan) it urges us to enjoy ourselves, because "Christmas comes but once a year." But he also composed the words of the beautiful "Rocking Hymn," set to music much later by Vaughan Williams. Simply written, but full of feeling, this Christmas favourite starts: "Sweet baby, sleep! What ails my dear? / What ails my darling thus to cry?" The Royalist Denham, for his part, was inspired by the views from a pleasant hill near Runnymede to write the prototypical English meditation on a nature. This was the much praised and imitated "Cooper's Hill," which would inspire Alexander Pope's similar meditation on nearby Windsor Forest in the next century.[2]

The sword and the quill are popular heraldic symbols, and Wither actually

The Sword and the Quill, heraldic device

sported them on his flag. After all, this was the first war in which propaganda played a major role, with the quill really being used as a weapon on both sides. Wither himself, a man of great conviction who had sold his estate to raise his cavalry brigade, had twice been imprisoned in the Marshalsea for his satirical verses, and had written political pamphlets as well. As for Denham, a judge's son who had been brought up on his father's Egham estate, his celebrated poem, first published that very year, isn't quite such a harmless meditation on Surrey scenery as it seems. For example, the site of nearby Chertsey Abbey, which was razed during the Reformation, fills him with foreboding: "may no such storm / Fall on our times, where ruin must reform" (lines 115–6). Of course, he had contemporary politics in mind here, and feared what King Charles's opponents might do in their overzealous

Puritanism. It was this kind of anxiety which had driven him to raise money for the king, who in return had made him Sheriff of the county.

So, while the might of the written word was being tested by the printing presses, these two poets had their own personal confrontation in Surrey. The story goes that Wither's defeat ended in a very gentlemanly way. Young Denham is said to have asked the king to spare the older man, explaining his generosity by joking, "While Wither lives, Denham will not be the worst poet in England"! But the anecdote hardly fits the facts.[3] Wither, this time, had avoided capture. He had escaped to Kingston with his stockpile of arms, leaving Denham's men to plunder his unguarded household, including his library. Besides, the pair's fortunes were quickly reversed. The parliament-arians returned within the month, and when they blew the main gate off the castle, it was Denham's turn to retreat. Wither duly put in a claim for compensation from him. So the harsh truth is that both men lost the castle without putting up a fight, and then did their best to ruin each other. Perhaps those who wield the pen should stick to it!

At least both Wither and Denham survived the war, Wither to become Cromwell's Major-General in Surrey, and Denham, in time, to become Charles II's Surveyor-General and to get a knighthood like his father before him. He was a friend of Evelyn's, and gave rise to one of the few humorous remarks in the famous diary when he wanted to have Greenwich Palace built right on the very edge of the Thames. Pure folly, thought Evelyn—"and so came away," he wrote smugly on 19 October 1661, "knowing Sir John to be a be a better poet than architect."

***

Surrey would be largely peaceful in the next few years, although Evelyn himself noted the skirmish at Surbiton in July 1648 which resulted in the death of a handsome young Royalist, Lord Francis Villiers, commemorated now in the names of Villiers Avenue, Villiers Close and Villiers Path, Surbiton. In the following year, too, there was a series of organised attacks on "The Diggers," non-violent activists who tried to assert their rights to common land at Weybridge. Ironically, the place they began cultivating, St George's Hill, is now something like the Beverly Hills of Surrey, a very elite residential area where only the very wealthiest (like Cliff Richard) can afford to live.

But it wasn't until later in the nineteenth century that the shadows of war really began to gather again. There was such fear of invasion then that a very distinguished military man called George Chesney, who was at that time setting up the Royal Indian Civil Engineering College on Cooper's Hill, wrote a short story about an imaginary one in the *Blackwood's Magazine* of May 1871. "The Battle of Dorking" is a disaster-story which predated Wells's *The War of the Worlds* and Jefferies' *After London*. Not exactly science fiction or fantasy, it is a call to action—a warning about the nation's lack of preparedness, told from the point of view of a poorly trained and ill-equipped volunteer facing German might. Like those other disturbing Surrey stories, it is all the more shocking for its pleasant setting. Although it was Chesney's very first attempt at fiction, it caused a sensation. Eventually, of course, his call for national conscription would have to be put into practice.

John Galsworthy

John Galsworthy, 1867–1933, in his study

First came the Crimean War, then the Boer Wars. Although the fighting was all far away, by the time of the Boer Wars a new breed of fearless war correspondents was bringing the fate of the British soldiers ever closer to the hearts of the civilians. John Galsworthy (1867–1933) was only a boy in Surrey when this conflict started. But as it entered its second phase, he came to understand its full horror, and expressed it memorably in the second book of his most important sequence of novels, *The Forsyte Saga*. A non-combatant himself, over the years he would nevertheless fight his own personal battle against triumphalism and war-mongering.

Galsworthy was born at Parkfield on Kingston Hill (now Galsworthy House, a nursing home) in August 1867, and brought up on nearby Coombe Hill, a favoured residential area with lovely views. In fact, his father, a solicitor, was responsible for the early development of Coombe Hill, for he bought a large acreage there and built three splendid houses on it, making a profit each time he sold up and moved on. The first, Coombe Warren, was demolished in 1931, but the other two still stand. Both are in use as schools now. The name of Coombe Croft is still etched into the stone gateposts of Rokeby School on George Road, while nearby Coombe Leigh, the impressively large and beautiful house where Galsworthy spent most of his

178

childhood, is now called Coombe Ridge and houses the Holy Cross Preparatory School. On one side of the school frontage is a cottage now named after the Robin Hill of *The Forsyte Saga*, and at the other end is the Coombe Wood golf course, giving at least partial access to the view from here. The Galsworthy family left to live in London in 1886 when the future writer was nineteen, but he went back to the area for inspiration, using it as an important part of the setting of his most famous work.

Coombe Leigh, now the Holy Cross Preparatory School, on Coombe Hill

"The site of the Forsyte House was the site of my father's Coombe Warren," he wrote later, "and the grounds and coppice, etc were actual, but the house itself I built with my imagination."[4] Here, he is clearly referring to the "odd sort of house" which the young architect Philip Bosinney builds at great expense for Soames Forsyte in the countryside at "Robin Hill" (*The Man of Property*, Chapter 8). When Soames first shows Bosinney the site, every detail rings true: the silvery river below them to the right, the typical Thames-basin gravelly soil, the smell of bracken from the thick woodland, and the beautiful sweep of the downs, almost blue in the summer sunshine.

Bosinney, stretching out under a great old oak, knows exactly the spot in which to build to get the best of the scenery. Clearly, it was a spot dear to the author himself. Galsworthy also identified the station that his characters use as Coombe and Malden. In Chapter 3, Part 3 of *In Chancery*, however, Surbiton Station is mentioned by name.

Galsworthy's Surrey childhood, and his father's series of building projects there, gave him more than just the setting of his best-known work. The whole long story unfolds from the feuds between Forsytes of the old school, with their obsession with property and possession, and those whose values are entirely different, and who adopt a freer lifestyle. Their feuds have dire consequences, not only for them but also for the next generation.

This is where the Boer War comes in, since Jolly, the son of Soames's bohemian cousin, Young Jolyon, is taunted into enlisting in the Boer War by his second cousin Val. Jolly in turn dares Val to enlist with him. Simply to prove his manhood (so much for the "honour" which drives men to war), Val agrees. The two young men's enlistment spurs Jolly's half-sister June and sister Holly to go out to South Africa as well, as nurses. As a result, *In Chancery*, first published in 1920, becomes the most powerful novelistic treatment of England during the Boer War.

The view from Coombe Hill

It is a bitter experience indeed. Young Jolyon's despair after seeing both his daughters off on the train from Surbiton (for Robin Hill has now come into his hands), and the subsequent unglamorous and lonely death of Jolly in a hospital bed, before he has even seen any action, confirm the general wretchedness and unheroic nature of war. Val, who marries his cousin Holly out there, isn't allowed to escape either: he gets a leg-wound. Not surprisingly, Galsworthy wrote in his diary on the eve of World War I:

> I hate and abhor war of all kinds; I despise and loathe it. And the thought of the million daily acts of its violence and hateful brutishness keeps riving my soul. I try not to think of all the poor creatures who are suffering and will suffer so terribly; but how not to? Wrote some words of Peace; but shan't send them anywhere. What's the use of whispering in the hurricane?

Looking back in the opening chapter of *To Let* (1921), Soames sees the Boer War as something "in the nature of a portent." Galsworthy was, in fact, torn in half by this new and larger-scale outbreak of conflict. He was very much against imperialism, but he was still deeply patriotic, as can be seen in his widely anthologised poem "England to Free Men":

I am your native land, who bred
No driven heart, no driven head;
I fly a flag in every sea
Round the old Earth, of Liberty!

He saw this new war as one that simply had to be fought, and although he argued against the harsh treatment of conscientious objectors, would not have been one himself (he was turned down by the army because of poor eyesight). He dutifully sends another batch of young Forsytes out to it, and this time two die, and one is wounded. But on the other hand, he longed for negotiations to end the war, and for a league of nations with peacekeeping forces. Having been invited, like H.G. Wells and many other writers of his day, to write for the hastily-formed War Propaganda Bureau,[5] he refused to fire off anti-enemy salvos. Instead, he used his "quill" to try to mitigate the effects of the "sword," by pleading for support for the wounded. An ardent humanist, he himself went out to France for a while, with his wife Ada, to help look after soldiers recovering from the after-effects of trench warfare. The couple also allowed their country home in the beautiful wilds of West Devon to be used as a convalescent home. When the war was over, Galsworthy objected publicly to war films which invariably covered up the truth about war, or glorified it. He particularly wanted the use of planes in warfare banned, foreseeing the horrific air-raids of World War II.

Although Galsworthy was a prolific writer of short stories, plays, essays and poems as well as novels, his reputation as a writer now rests on *The Forsyte Saga*, which was published in one volume in 1922. Like Forster's novels, this has had a whole new lease of life (several times now) as a result of film and radio adaptations. The most popular of all was the television serial of 1967. However, remakes have also had big audiences, not only in England but all over the world. The 1990 BBC radio serial stretched to twenty-three parts, and was the most expensive one ever produced. It was rerun in 2004.

Galsworthy may not have been avant-garde or profound, but his analysis of the English class system, and his panoramic view of English life from the late Victorian to the inter-war years, have never lost their fascination. In particular, few have expressed as memorably as Galsworthy the dreadful conflict between the need to possess and the desire for freedom, a conflict which is reflected outwards from the individual into the social, political and even world order. His general conclusion, of course, is that possession must always elude us. On the purely personal level, the central figure of the saga, that quintessential "man of property" Soames Forsyte, is not allowed a son and heir, and his adored daughter Fleur cannot remain "his" either. It's left to Fleur's husband Michael to say, in the penultimate paragraph of *Swan Song* (1928), "To have and to hold! As though you could!"

In 1917, Galsworthy had rejected a knighthood, like Evelyn and Wells before him, feeling that writers should not accept titles. When he was awarded the Nobel Prize for Literature in 1932, he was already ill because of the brain tumour which would soon kill him. He had always been extremely generous with his income, and now he gave the whole of the prize money away to charity. After his death, more of his charitable donations came to light. In these ways, Galsworthy to a large extent won his own battle with the all too human desire to possess.

Warwick Deeping

Another immensely prolific and popular novelist whose work was touched by war moved to Surrey in 1919 and spent the rest of his life here. This was Warwick Deeping (1877–1950), who had been a doctor in the trenches. He lived at Eastlands, a large house in Weybridge, once the home of the Regency actress Fanny Kemble. Like Galsworthy, Deeping is by no means confined to the category of war writer. Yet for him, as for Galsworthy, war was far more than mere background material.

Deeping himself often declared that it was his experience in the trenches that brought his work closer to reality, and his best-known novel, *Sorrell and Son* (1925), captured the public imagination by dealing with the post-war tribulations of Captain Stephen Sorrell, MC. It's a touching

Warwick Deeping, 1877–1950, around the beginning of the twentieth century

story in which Sorrell, having come through the war as a hero, sacrifices everything for his son Christopher's future. The feeling between father and son is established early in the book, when Christopher says, "you will still be Captain Sorrell, M.C., to me, daddy. If you swept the streets—." "Honor bright?" asks Sorrell, anxious for reassurance. "Honor bright," says the boy, getting a hug from his father in return (Chapter 4). This mixture of harsh reality and tenderness is characteristic of Deeping's work, and he found just the right medium for it in the historical romance, his first and last love as a writer. His swansong was *The Sword and the Cross* (1950), which deals with ancient Britain during the upheavals of the fifth century.

Such upheavals evidently gave Deeping the opportunity to explore the darker side of life, and the extremes of emotion, in ways which were acceptable to the masses. They responded by snapping up his books. As a result, he was a household name in the twenties and thirties, in a way that

Forster, for instance, never was. For example, in 1937 he was featured on a popular series of Wills cigarette cards as one of the "Famous British Authors." And he deserved his fame. Despite criticisms of him as lowbrow, sensationalist, sentimental and so on (in other words, "popular"), he had some very illustrious supporters in the literary world, and was certainly capable of telling a gripping story and moving the heart.

There are some good descriptive passages in his novels, too, and some of these are about Surrey. After all, he wrote all his best work from here. *Corn in Egypt* (1941), for example, is a Surrey novel which deals with a typically lower-middle-class hero who falls in love with tumbledown Blackthorn Farm by the Pilgrims' Way, buys it up, and then struggles to make a go of it. His worst experience comes at the end, during the Second World War. The village is full of evacuees from London and the South coast, but it does not escape the bombing, and his wife Phillida is badly injured—paralysed, in fact. Nevertheless, at the end of the last chapter he summons up the courage to go forward with her, helping her to adjust, and, as far as possible, allowing her to help him: "I was part of an old and steadfast world," he tells himself, "part of time. This little valley would be here, fruitful and good, long after my feet had passed, and the evil genius of man had tired of its foul new toys." Incidentally, during this period, Deeping himself had turned his grounds into market gardens, donating their produce to the war effort.

As for *The Sword and the Cross*, that is set in the "hill country south of Londinium in a valley between the heaths and the downland." On one occasion, his hero, Gerontius, crosses the Thames at what is clearly the ford at Cowey Sale near Walton Bridge.

Here, then, is someone who was very much a local author, and one who achieved an enormous following in the troubled years before and after World War II. He deserves to be remembered as (at the very least) a chronicler of social change, and there are many who feel that his achievement goes much further than that. When he died, his ashes were scattered in the Garden of Remembrance at Woking Crematorium, and his house came into the hands of the National Trust, who later leased it out as a private home.

Siegfried Sassoon

Now, however, it's time to look at someone who is really known as a war writer. Indeed, Galsworthy had asked him to contribute something to his short-lived wartime periodical, *Reveille*—an excellent choice, because no one has ever had a sharper "quill" in writing about war than Siegfried Sassoon (1886–1967).

Sassoon's link with Surrey is the most tenuous of any of the authors dealt with here, yet it affected him very deeply. The story of it reads like a chapter of Galsworthy's own saga, for it is the tale of a painful disinheritance. As so often, though, fact is even stranger than fiction.

The Sassoons were Sephardic Jews from the Middle East, who had been doing business in India. Sassoon's grandfather was actually born in Bombay. But he came to London in 1858, to manage the family's business there, and, like so many rich businessmen working in London, found himself a country estate in Surrey. The estate, originally a vast mansion built on land belonging to Hampton Court Palace, had splendid grounds with a fine sweeping drive, part of which can still be traced by the line of the trees. But, despite a few concessions to their new culture, the family seem to have clung to their past. Perhaps this is symbolised by the coat of arms designed in consultation with the family in 1862: amongst its features were a lion of Judah, a palm tree and a pomegranate. No wonder, then, that Sassoon's grandmother was horrified when her son Alfred fell in love with Theresa Thornycroft, a Gentile girl—a sculptor's daughter at that, and eight years older than he was. Sassoon's grandfather had died by then, and under the terms of his will, Alfred could not actually be disinherited. However, when the young couple got married secretly in Kensington in 1884, Alfred's mother wanted nothing more to do with them, and forbade the rest of the family to have anything to do with them, either. Siegfried was born in 1886, the couple's second child, with Middle Eastern blood running through his veins, and the weight of a family feud on his shoulders.[6]

Siegfried Sassoon, 1886–1967, in 1916 (© Imperial War Museum)

As a child, he was not, in fact, completely cut off from the Surrey Sassoons. Alfred's sister Rachel (who would also marry a non-Jew) had been friendly with Theresa, and went on seeing her. This continued even after Alfred left his wife and children, something that happened when Siegfried was only five. The young boy's visits to his Aunt Rachel's luxurious house in Mayfair were very memorable, and he was fond of this lively woman who took him and his brothers to matinees at the opera and theatre. Then, when he was seven, he finally met his Ashley Park grandmother. His father, whom he still adored, was dying of tuberculosis, and the old woman relented. She and her other son came to the deathbed. Sassoon felt that she looked quite foreign, and was uncomfortable when she showed him the family tree: the Sassoons considered themselves to be descendants of the original King David, which must have seemed a very big and startling claim to a small boy who knew his Bible. He wrote more than forty years later that:

> it comes back to me, that sense of being among strangers, with 'Pappy' being killed by that terrible cough, and the queer feeling that although this new Grandmamma was making such a fuss of us, it would make no difference if we never saw her again …. And I remember my miserable feeling that the only thing which mattered was that my mother ought to be there, and that these people were unfriendly to her who loved my father as they had never done and would have come to him with unquestioning forgiveness.[7]

Grandma Sassoon is one of just a few unkind portraits in Sassoon's childhood reminiscences in *Old Century* (1938). Actually, he never did see either of those two Sassoons again, since he was too upset to go to his father's funeral: "it seemed as though our father had been taken away from us by strangers," he wrote.[8]

More happily, Sassoon had met his great-aunt, his paternal grandfather's youngest sister, at Rachel's house. As he recalled in *The Weald of Youth* (1942), he met her again in his twenties, and struck up a real friendship with her. She talked to him about the family in more detail, and made them seem less alien to him, more human and familiar. Perhaps that was why, later on, he was able to accept that side of himself better, and credit it with some part of his special poetic genius:

> the daemon in me is Jewish. And as a poetic spirit I have always felt myself—or wanted to be—a kind of minor prophet. I suppose most poets aim at being prophetic communicators. But the idea has always been very strong in my mind. And found utterance in the war poems, of course.[9]

Sassoon's preoccupation with death, his sense of loss, and his even stronger sense of justice, may all have been conditioned by this early experience.

Here he is, for example, in "The General," one of his most frequently anthologised poems about the fighting in France, railing against the superficial bonhomie and dreadful incompetence of the top brass in the army. It's all done in a couple of tiny snapshots, with two scraps of speech. First, the General greets the troops heartily on the morning of the offensive, then two of the men are overheard commenting on the greeting:

> "He's a cheery old card," grunted Harry to Jack
> As they slogged up to Arras with rifle and pack.

The verbs "grunted" and "slogged" are more than enough to recreate the scene here. Then comes a blank line, a pause, not so much for reflection as for imagining the fate which awaits Harry, Jack and so many others—a fate confirmed by one last line:

> But he did for them both by his plan of attack.

And that's all. Nothing more is said. Yet these simple words carry the poet's own judgement, putting the blame squarely on the General's shoulders, and leaving us with a bitter question. How could this "old card" have sent these young men to their doom so cheerfully, so carelessly?

Part of the old gateway to Ashley Park

Sassoon was actually invited to visit Ashley Park once, after he won the Military Cross in France in 1916. But he didn't go. Instead, he went on to make his famous "Statement," a defiant protest against the war, and threw his ribbon into the mouth of the River Mersey. His only visit, if it can be called that, was the one with Forster in 1923, just to look at the old house before it was demolished. In his diary entry for the day, he recalls having twice seen the last occupant of the house, his reclusive uncle Joseph, but gives no details about the meetings. He has been very much enjoying his stay with the Forsters at Harnham, giving affectionate and amusing details about their rather quaint household, but once he stands in front of the Ashley Park mansion, his tone changes. He is particularly scathing about the coat of arms over the door. Not mentioning its exoticism, he calls it simply "such a shoddy piece of work that already (after only seventy years) it is sagging outwards, as if protesting that it was too hastily concocted by the Heralds' College."[10] Evidently, he didn't think much of the family's credentials or pretensions.

There's really no doubt that this poet's keen sense of justice (or rather, injustice) was fired not only by his Jewish blood, but also by the way his mother, in particular, was treated by her Surrey in-laws.

R.C. Sherriff

R.C. Sherriff, 1896–1975, coaching a crew on the Thames

There could be no better way to end both chapter and book than with a totally unpretentious Esher resident whose war-writing reached incredible heights of fame—and who bequeathed his Surrey estate to be used for the arts.

The story of Robert Cedric Sherriff (1896–1975) is an amazing one. Born at Hampton Wick, Bob, as he preferred to be called, went to Kingston Grammar School, and like his father before him took up a career in the insurance business. After his war service as the captain of a Surrey regiment in France and Belgium, he returned to his job, and to the sport he particularly loved—rowing. In fact, he tells us in his autobiography that he used his "wounds gratuity" to buy a sculling boat.[11] Soon, he had a new hobby: writing for the Kingston Rowing Club's fund-raising shows. "Rowing and writing went well together," he discovered, recalling this process with a lyrical simplicity:

> There was music in the rhythm of a racing boat when the crew was on balance, rowing their blades in hard and true. You felt the boat leap forward as the stroke was driven through, and then, as the crew swung forward, the boat seemed to float on air and the rhythm sang

187

to you while everything was at peace and rest. On a long outing on a fine still day, with the river as smooth as glass, the physical part of you would blend so smoothly with the rest of the crew that you ceased to be conscious of a separate body and the mind was free to take wings of its own.

Nearly ten years later, in 1928, he turned this new hobby to good account by writing a play called *Journey's End*. It wasn't one of the fund-raisers, as is sometimes supposed. That phase of his life was over now. Rather, it was an antidote to the boredom of his job, and a way of easing "the itch to write something of my own" which those amateur theatricals had awakened in him. It also made use of two characters from an earlier attempt at novel-writing, and drew on his own letters home from the front. As sometimes happens, everything came together to create a landmark work. A single Sunday night /Monday matinee staging of the play, with the young Laurence Olivier in the starring role, was enough to bring it to the critics' attention. George Bernard Shaw also helped it on its way to becoming a massive world-wide hit. This led to a brilliant Hollywood career for Sherriff, who wrote the screenplays for (amongst others) Wells's *Invisible Man* (1933), *Goodbye, Mr Chips* (1939) and *The Dambusters* (1943).

In *Journey's End*, the play which catapulted Sherriff to fame, Olivier played Stanhope, a dashing army captain. Stanhope still has many fine qualities, but his nerves are so shattered by three years of gruelling war experience that he can only keep going by drinking. To his dismay, the new officer sent out to join the company is young Raleigh, who had idolised him at school, and whose sister Madge is his "girl." (Stanhope and Raleigh were the two characters from Sherriff's discarded novel.) A German attack is imminent, and the threat of death is ever-present, but what troubles Stanhope now is what Raleigh might say about him when he writes home. Considering the circumstances, this concern is irrelevant. Yet it is, of course, profoundly human.

Other characters in the play include Stanhope's second-in-command, a sympathetic middle-aged schoolmaster who puts him to bed at night when he gets drunk, another officer who has virtually lost the battle with his nerves, and a cheery, portly salt-of-the-earth second-lieutenant. The audience cares about each and every one of them, and suffers with them as their personal dramas unfold in their miserable dugout in the trenches. Fear, nostalgia, humour both real and faked, the awkwardness of trying to "rub along" with different types of people at such close quarters and in this hierarchical set-up—these all help to make an utterly authentic picture of men reacting variously to the terrible stresses of war. The tension never lapses, and the ending, in which Raleigh is fatally wounded and Stanhope stumbles up the dugout stairs as heavy fire reduces it to rubble behind him, is almost unbearable. No wonder its first audience sat in silence at the end of the performance, taking time to recover (or put away their handkerchiefs) before remembering to applaud.

Yet Sherriff wasn't an anti-war writer in the sense that Sassoon was. He confessed that, as a young man, he had thrown himself into the war with a sense of release from everyday drudgery, as had so many young men of that time, including Rupert Brooke. He had enjoyed the training in England, and even in his autobiography makes only the most glancing mention of the "bad times in France." Not only did he never protest against the war in his own voice, as Sassoon did, but he also remained fiercely proud of his regiment, the East Surreys, which was indeed renowned for its fighting spirit.[12] So this isn't a simple diatribe against war. No one is actually killed on stage here. Action centres round the regular production of meals by the officers' cook, visits by the colonel, and the coming and going of men to the line. Stanhope's sarcasm when speaking to the colonel is quickly brushed aside by the colonel himself ("Don't be silly, Stanhope," Act III, scene i). Later, his face remains a blank when the colonel more or less admits that he expected casualties from a raid. Indeed, an army major who recently took fifty riflemen to see the current West End production of *Journey's End* was very pleased that he had brought his men to see the play. He commented afterwards that "it was the best thing they had done in the army,"[13] perhaps feeling that it would promote understanding and comradeship among his men, and encourage them to stand by each other even in the worst situation. He didn't seem to think that it would turn the men into pacifists.

However, "the bad times in France" must have bitten deep into Sherriff's sensitive soul. The wider implications of the play are quite clear. The schoolmaster officer reads out loud from *Alice in Wonderland* just before he meets his death. "I don't see no point in that," says the cockney second-lieutenant who listens to a bit of one of the nonsense poems. "Exactly," says the other, "That's just the point" (Act II, Scene ii). In writing about the folly and nightmarish horror of war, and of how it pushes men to the breaking-point, Sherriff has presented a powerful argument against war-mongering. And that argument is as powerful and, sadly, as relevant today as it ever was. Movingly, Sherriff also shows how the human spirit can rise above even the most incredible pressures. Stanhope, for example, acquits himself well in the end, and does not let the hero-worshipping Raleigh down after all. In these ways, Sherriff proved yet again that the pen (or the quill) really is mightier than the sword.

One particular reason that the latest production of *Journey's End* is running to packed houses is that the play is currently on the National Curriculum. It was an inspired choice, for nothing could show children the ultimate futility and waste of war more poignantly than Raleigh's brief, bitter initiation into it.

Sherriff's voice is still being heard in another way, too. After retiring from Hollywood screen writing, he returned to Esher again to live quietly in Rosebriars, the dream home with rose-garden, orchard and so on which he had bought for himself and his parents in his early thirties, with part of the proceeds of *Journey's End*. He had sometimes worried about how to keep it running, and had always hated to leave it, even for Hollywood, especially when the flowers were in bloom. In his will, he left the estate to the community, for the benefit of the arts, and it was sold in 1993 to produce the R.C. Sherriff Rosebriars Trust. The fund, currently administered from Walton-on-Thames, supports a variety of arts programmes for schools, brings concerts to local venues such as the nearby hospice, underwrites cultural events in the borough, allows young artists of all kinds to go to summer schools or on other short courses, and so forth.

The R.C. Sherriff Rosebriars Trust logo

****

As the usefulness of the R.C. Sherriff Rosebriars Trust suggests, the arts continue to flourish here in Surrey, right from the grassroots upwards. J.G. Ballard and Jacqueline Wilson, authors who have shown great attachment to their homes here, and who are currently pre-eminent in their own genres, have already been mentioned. Another important figure on the contemporary literary scene also owes much to his Surrey years: Booker-prizewinning "literary" novelist Kazuo Ishiguro confessed to Mark Lawson on BBC4's "Front Row" programme on 17 February 2005 that he was "quite amazed" at the "great kindness" with which he and his family were treated when they came to Guildford from Japan in 1960, a mere fifteen years after the end of the war. Ishiguro, who was only six years old then, found his "exotic origin" no bar to enjoying his new life, and settled easily into his schools, first in Guildford and then in Woking. Proof of his solid grounding in home-counties' England is provided by the quintessentially English subject of his most celebrated novel to date, *The Remains of the Day* (1989)—the perfect butler.[14]

So, you see, the story of "Literary Surrey" is not finished yet.

Notes to Chapter 10

[1] George Herbert Clarke was an eminent English-born scholar, poet and editor who was to become a Fellow of the Royal Society of Canada. His 1917 *Treasury of War Poetry*, which included two of his own poems, was very well received. The sentimental Georgian-style poem printed here, evidently written while enjoying a visit to his native land, is very much of its time. "He who believes that peace is illusory and spurious, unless it is based upon justice and liberty, will be proud to battle," says Clarke in his introduction, "if battle he must, for the sake of these foundations"—a typical perspective at this time.

190

[2] This poem too has some connection with war, having been expanded from an earlier version to celebrate the Treaties of Utrecht (1713–14), marking the end of the Spanish War of Succession. The poem ends hopefully with a vision of the Thames open to a world at peace. Not long afterwards, Pope came to live on the banks of the Thames himself, at Twickenham (now in the London Borough of Richmond and Twickenham). Here he built himself a splendid villa with elaborate gardens and a remarkable underground grotto.

[3] See Matthew Alexander's *More Surrey Tales*, Newbury: Countryside, 1986, p.46. As the curator of the Guildford Museum, Matthew Alexander could hardly be a more reliable source.

[4] See H.V. Marrot's *The Life and Letters of John Galsworthy*, London: Heinemann, 1935. Later quotations in this section are all from this edition unless otherwise specified.

[5] He wasn't really in sympathy with the project, but he used it for his own purposes. See his article, "Literature and Propaganda." in *Glimpses and Reflections*, London: Heinemann, 1937, pp.167–9.

[6] Talking of "his relationship to the world that existed before he was born and those events he was too young to remember," John Stuart Roberts writes, "Here is the seed-corn from which grew the major themes of his poetry and prose," *Siegfried Sassoon, 1886–1967*, London: Richard Cohen Books, 1999, p.16. It certainly seems significant that in his semi-autobiographical work, Sassoon actually sees himself as an isolated, lonely orphan. *Memoirs of a Fox-Hunting Man* opens, "My childhood was a queer and not altogether happy one" (London: Faber 1975). The psychological impact of the Sassoons' rejection seems to have been huge.

[7] *The Old Century and Seven Years*, quoted by Jean Moorcroft Wilson, *The Making of a War Poet: A Biography, 1886–1918*, London: Duckworth, 1998, p.48.

[8] Quoted by Wilson, p.50.

[9] *Siegfried Sassoon: Poet's Pilgrimage*, ed. Dame Felicitas Corrigan, London: Victor Gollancz, 1973, p.47.

[10] *Diaries, 1923–1925*, edited Rupert Hart-Davis, London: Faber, 1985, p.50. I am indebted to Michael Dane for helping me to locate the spot where the two writers would probably have stood.

[11] *No Leading Lady: An Autobiography*, London: Gollancz, 1968. Later quotations in this section are all from this edition unless otherwise specified.

[12] Quoted by Robert Gore-Langton in "Truth from the Trenches," *The Spectator*, 15 January 2005, p.20. Please note, there are some other factual errors in this article (apart from the myth that *Journey's End* was offered to the Kingston Rowing Club for one of its "shows"). For instance, Rosebriars wasn't "promptly demolished" after Sherriff's death. And "Esher's great warrior writer" isn't "long forgotten," certainly not in the borough of Elmbridge!

[13] One testimony to this is the anonymous poem, "The Game," discussed by Paul Fussell in *The Great War and Modern Memory* (Oxford: Oxford University Press, 1980), pp.27–28. It tells the story of a company of the East Surreys who kept focussed by dribbling footballs "through a hail of slaughter" into the enemy trenches. The first stanza ends, "True to the land that bore them / The SURREYS play the game."

[14] Coincidentally, the most famous of all literary butlers, Jeeves, was also created by

a novelist with a Guildford connection. P.G. Wodehouse was born at what is now 59 Epsom Road, Guildford, in 1881, while his mother was staying with her sister there.

Suggested Reading

1. Poems and extracts of poems by George Wither and John Denham in *The New Oxford Book of Seventeenth-Century Verse*, edited by Alastair Fowler, Oxford: Oxford University Press, 1991. The extract from Denham's "Cooper's Hill," about the Thames near Chertsey, contains the lines quoted here and ends with the famous passage, "Oh could I flow like thee, and make thy stream / My great example, as it is my theme! / Though deep, yet clear, though gentle, yet not dull, / Strong without rage, without o'erflowing full" (lines 189–992).
2. Very appropriately, the words of "Wither's Rocking Hymn" can be found on the web at <www.allsaintskingston.co.uk/music/anthems/v.htm>
3. John Galsworthy's *Forsyte Saga*, Ware: Wordsworth Classics, 1994 (a good long read!)
4. James Gindin's *John Galsworthy's Life and Art*, London: Macmillan, 1987. Plate 3 shows "one of the houses at Coombe" as it was then, in an unbelievably rural setting.
5. Siegfried Sassoon, *The War Poems*, London: Faber, 1983.
6. Sassoon's *Memoirs of a Fox-Hunting Man* (see note 6 above). The title sounds all the more nostalgic now. See Chapter 5 for the young hero's rather disastrous first hunt!
7. Michael Dane's *The Sassoons of Ashley Park* (Walton-on-Thames: Michael Dane, 1999).
8. R.C. Sherriff's *Journey's End*, Harmondsworth: Penguin, 1983.

Places to Visit

Farnham Castle, once held by Civil War poets of opposing sides, is in walking distance of Farnham Station just overlooking the town centre. See "Places to Visit" for Cobbett, at the end of Chapter 3 above.

John Denham's Cooper's Hill, with the Magna Carta Memorial at its foot and the John F. Kennedy and (British and Commonwealth) Air Force Memorial on its slopes, is very much on the tourist track. The engineering college which Sir George Chesney founded is now part of Brunel University's campus there. The National Trust owns much of the area. The nearest station is Egham.

Alexander Pope's Grotto (see note 2 above) remains, even though his villa was demolished. It now lies under buildings used by St James's Independent School for Boys, Twickenham, TW1 4QG. This extraordinary creation can be seen on Open Days, or by written application to the school. For details of Open Days see

Coombe Hill, where Galsworthy spent his childhood, is just off Kingston Hill coming out of Kingston towards London. Rokeby School (the old Coombe Croft) and the Holy Cross School (the old Coombe Leigh) are both on George Road, which runs through the Coombe Wood Golf Club's golf-course. The nearest station is Norbiton.

Walton-on-Thames still has some reminders of the original Ashley Park estate, mainly in road names, some fine old trees, Great Gates (the cottage on the roundabout of Ashley Road, now a beautician's), and the original posts marking the "short drive" to the house just off Ashley Park Avenue. Further in, on a little green beside a huge plane tree, one side of the old gatepost has been preserved as a feature. Sassoon Cottages, at the top of Cottimore Crescent, off Cottimore Lane on the other side of the town centre, are the only buildings which still bear the family name.

Eastlands, where Warwick Deeping lived, is on Brooklands Lane, Weybridge, not far from the station. However, privacy is an issue in this location. Anyone interested in Deeping should contact the Warwick Deeping Appreciation Society at <www.sndc.demon.co.uk/wdsubs.htm>.

Rosebriars, where Sherriff lived in Esher, is remembered in the name of a very pleasant housing development off Esher Park Lane behind Esher Library, which occupies that land—and, of course, in the R.C. Sherriff Rosebriars Trust, administered from Case House on the High Street of Walton-on-Thames.

*__The Savoy Chapel__ in London, tucked away behind the Strand to the right of the Savoy Hotel, is where George Wither was buried. Although Wither's remains were inadvertently cremated when the chapel burnt down in the nineteenth century, a picture of him is kept there (you will need to ask to see it). There are also connections with Chaucer and Pepys. This beautiful little royal chapel with its illustrious history is well worth a visit. Open 11.30am–3.30pm every weekday except Monday. Incidentally, the picture again shows Wither with a very finely worked collar, suggesting that he wasn't a strict Puritan by nature.

Note about the author

Jacqueline Banerjee received her BA and PhD degrees from King's College, London, and has been a Research Fellow at Lucy Cavendish College, Cambridge. She has taught English Literature at universities in England, Canada, Ghana and Japan, and publishes regularly in scholarly journals, newspapers and magazines. Her two previous books are *Through the Northern Gate: Childhood and Growing Up in British Fiction, 1719–1901* (1996), and *Paul Scott* (1999). Now home in Surrey again, she loves treading in the footsteps of some of her favourite authors.

ᘓᘓᘓ

Other books of interest: from the same publisher—

The Hilltop Writers—a Victorian Colony among the Surrey Hills, by W.R. Trotter. Rich in detail yet thoroughly readable, this book tells of sixty-six writers including Tennyson, Conan Doyle and George Bernard Shaw who chose to work among the hills around Haslemere and Hindhead in the last decades of the 19th century.
ISBN 1-873855-31-1 March 2003, paperback, 260pp, illustrations and maps.

Heatherley—by Flora Thompson—her sequel to the 'Lark Rise' trilogy. The book which Flora Thompson wrote about her time in the area where the counties of Hampshire, Surrey and Sussex meet. It is the 'missing' fourth part to her *Lark Rise to Candleford* in which 'Laura Goes Further.' Full of interest to those who know this area. Illustrated with chapter-heading line drawings by Hester Whittle. Introduction by Ann Mallinson.
ISBN 1-873855-29-X Sept 1998, notes revised 2005, paperback, 176pp, includes map.

John Owen Smith, publisher:—
www.johnowensmith.co.uk/books

Index